26.2 LIFE LESSONS

Helping You Keep Pace with the Marathon of Life

Cami Ostman, M.S.
Carol Frazey, M.S.

26.2 LIFE LESSONS

Helping You Keep Pace with the Marathon of Life

Cami Ostman, M.S.
Carol Frazey, M.S.

Sidekick Press
Bellingham, Washington

Sidekick Press
2950 Newmarket Street
Suite 101-329
Bellingham, Washington 98226
www.sidekickpress.com

26.2 Life Lessons: Helping You Keep Pace with the Marathon of Life
ISBN 978-1-7369351-1-8
LCCN 2021919259

Cover Image: Jolene Hanson
Cover Design: Spoken Design (spokendesign.com)

Information in this book and from Fit School, Inc., Carol Frazey, and/or Cami Ostman should not be used to alter a medically prescribed regimen or as a form of self-treatment. Consult a licensed physician before beginning this or any other exercise and/or nutrition program.

To our badass clients!

"Running has given me the courage to start, the determination to keep trying, and the childlike spirit to have fun along the way. Run often and run long, but never outrun your joy of running."

—Julie Isphording, marathon-winner

CONTENTS

About This Book

We, Carol and Cami, are two women who come at running from two different but complementary perspectives. Carol has been running since her adolescence and can be said to understand the craft and form of what it takes to turn oneself into an efficient runner. With a master's degree in Kinesiology, she has a deep knowledge of how the body works and what one needs to do, physically and psychologically, to improve its performance. She has a solid grasp on what good nutrition looks like and really walks the walk (or runs the run, as the case may be) in her own life. Cami came to running late—in her mid-thirties. Her first forays into long-distance training occurred during her divorce and, thus, she approaches her running life as a metaphor: What does running teach us about how to live our lives? As a family therapist, Cami's perspective tends toward the "heart and soul" of running, the catharsis and power it has to deepen us.

But we both agree on this: Running has changed our lives. We've had numerous coach/therapist discussions about how all women, no matter their ability level, could benefit from running (or walking), if only they could see in the sport what we see. That's why we've put this book together.

Here you have a compilation of Cami's reflections from blogs and articles, mostly on running as metaphor, alternating with Carol's coaching tips on how to bring intention and improvement to your running and eating.

Ultimately, this book can be used as a twenty-six-week training program to get you ready for a marathon.

This little volume is a gift for those of you who have participated in one of our challenges or programs over the past few years—and for those of you we have yet to encounter. We want to thank you for joining in—moving your bodies, growing as people, and learning to embrace life.

Enjoy.

How to Use the Running Program

This program is intended to make your life better: physically, psychologically, and nutritionally. When we focus on the connection of our inner world with our physical bodies, great things can happen.

Each week, you are given an essay from Cami to read and reflect on. Then you are given an intention word, reflection, mantra, running focus, weekly workout, and nutrition goal from Carol.

Below are explanations of the different weekly sections and how to use them.

Intention Word: Use this word as a focus point to stay mindful during the week.

Reflection: Answer the reflection questions in your mind or write your answers down. These questions will help you look inward and consider what is really important to you.

Mantra: Repeat this mantra during your runs on the week that is indicated. Pay attention to how you feel at the end of each week after repeating a positive mantra consistently during your workouts.

Running Focus: Each week, you will be asked to focus on one running habit. The tips in this section will help you improve your form, develop a racing mindset, improve your running breathing, and live a healthier lifestyle.

Description of Workouts and Definition of Terms

The daily workouts, if you follow them faithfully, will ultimately get you trained and ready for a marathon. By consistently following a plan that includes a speed workout, tempo or pace workout, and a long run each week, you develop a strong foundation for running the marathon distance.

Your first workout will be a **Benchmark Time-Trial**. This is to test what type of walking/running shape you are in. This information will be the baseline for all of your subsequent workouts.

The **One Mile Time-Trial** (or 1600 meters) is equal to four times around a standard running track. During this workout, you will time yourself and write this time down to use as your baseline.

Speed Workout: During speed workouts, you will focus on turn-over. Turn-over is how fast you pick your foot up off the ground and put it back down again.

Hill/Strength Workout: By running up hills, you gain strength in your muscles differently from what you achieve with flat-land running.

Consistent Speed as Distance Increases: During these workouts, you will keep the same pace whether you are running for one minute or six minutes. These workouts teach you how to hold a consistent pace.

Pacing Workout: These workouts teach you how to hold a steady, consistent pace for an entire run or race.

Tempo Workout: When doing tempo workouts, you are pushing a little bit harder for a longer period of time. Your goal is to keep a consistent, quick pace for the entire time.

Goal Race Pace Workout: To find your Goal Marathon Pace, add three minutes to your 1-Mile Time Trial Pace.

Taper: A taper is when you are decreasing your running mileage before a race so that you are rested and ready to run.

Cross Training: These are any workouts that are not walking or running, including cycling, kayaking, rollerblading, elliptical walking, cross-country skiing, swimming, yoga, or any other activity that uses different muscle groups.

Long Run: When training for a marathon, the long run is the most important run each week. You are teaching your body and mind to run longer and longer distances. Your long runs should be relaxed and slower than what we are going to call your "Comfortably Hard" pace. Find a pace where you can talk throughout the entire run. If you are not sure where to start, start out at a pace that is 30 seconds slower than your marathon pace (see below for calculation).

Calculating 1-Mile Pace

My 1-Mile Time =   _____

Date: _____

1-Mile Lap Pace (400 meters) = My 1-Mile Time ÷ 4 =   _____

Finishing time for Lap 1   _____

Finishing time for Lap 2 (if you stay on pace)   _____

Finishing time for Lap 3 (if you stay on pace)   _____

Finishing time for Lap 4 (if you stay on pace)   _____

Example: Calculating 1-Mile Pace

My 1-Mile Time =	9:52
1-Mile Lap Pace (400 meters) = My 1-Mile Time ÷ 4 =	2:28/lap
Lap 1 = 2:28	2:28
Lap 2 = (2:28 + 2:28)	4:56
Lap 3 = (2:28 + 2:28 + 2:28)	7:24
Lap 4 = (2:28 + 2:28 + 2:28 + 2:28)	9:52

Calculating a 5K/Comfortably Hard (CH) Pace

My 1-Mile Time Trial + 40 seconds = my 5K/CH Pace _____

CH Pace ÷ 4 = _____

Your CH Pace for each 400 meters (1 lap of a standard running track)

Lap 1 finishing time: _____

Lap 2 finishing time: _____

Lap 3 finishing time: _____

Lap 4 finishing time: _____

Example: Calculating 5K/Comfortably Hard (CH) Pace

My 1-Mile Time Trial (9:52) + 40 seconds = CH Pace   10:32

CH Pace (10:32) ÷ 4 =   2:38

Your CH Pace for each 400 meters (1 lap of a standard running track—this is also the pace you eventually maintain for a full 5K)

Lap 1 = 2:38   2:38

Lap 2 = 2:38 + 2:38   5:16

Lap 3 = 2:38 + 2:38 + 2:38   7:54

Lap 4 = 2:38 + 2:38 + 2:38 + 2:38   10:32

Calculating Goal Race Pace for a Marathon

1-Mile Time + 3 minutes = Goal Pace for Marathon _____

Calculating Your Goal Race Pace for the Marathon Example

1-Mile Time (9:52) + 3 minutes = 12:52 Goal Race Pace for Your Marathon (the pace you would keep for each mile of your goal marathon race).

Nutrition Goal

Nutrition is a large component of your healthy lifestyle. Take time each week to integrate each chapter's nutrition goals into your life as a way of becoming more conscious of the food that you are putting into your body.

Note from Carol on the Philosophy of Running and Racing Workouts

These workouts are for any level of runner from beginner to elite. Since all of the workouts are based on your own individual pace, runners of all levels can benefit. The Long Run days increase gradually to reduce the risk of injury.

Having been a runner for almost forty years, I've had the experience of being a runner at every level. I learned running basics as a thirteen-year-old cross-country and track runner. I was fortunate enough to run competitively at the Division 1 level at Penn State University. I was also fortunate enough to start running again VERY slowly after gaining forty-two pounds when I was pregnant with my first child and then sixty-four pounds with my second! As one wise woman commented, "You know, babies only weigh about seven to nine pounds when they are born!" It took me about two years after the birth of each of my children to get back to my "fighting weight," but it was worth the effort.

Whether you are in "just maintaining a healthy lifestyle mode" or "racing mode," you can still do the same Speed and Pacing Workouts that I am sharing with you in this book. The only thing different for each runner will be the pace. The intensity will feel the same because you are basing your pace on your current 1-Mile Time Trial Pace. If you focus on the important three workouts (speed day, tempo/pace day, and long run), you can have the best racing times of your life. My belief is that the other days are "filler." Putting intensity into the main three workouts rather than merely putting in more miles each week is how everyone can improve. I've used this training to run my own best marathon (in 3:28), and now I share it with you so that you can run your first or best marathon. As Cami shares her insights into maintaining a healthy psychology for using running as a foundation for how to BE a strong, healthy human, Carol offers the training program as a path to achieving your best running ever. Good luck!

Running Reflections: Crisis or Chance to Live Your Passion?

Wikipedia describes a midlife crisis as a period of "dramatic self-doubt that is felt by some individuals during the 'middle years' or middle age of life." Personally, as I (Cami) work with individuals in workshops, therapy, and coaching, I see less self-doubt than reevaluation when people reach transition points. If we're lucky, "midlife" goes on for a good long time, and we're bound to ask ourselves whether or not the foundations we've built in our young adult years are sustainable as we move forward. Those of us who are seeking a proverbial second wind are trying to find our stride—a stride that feels good for our bodies and our ever-changing lives.

My personal entry into the numerous transitions midlife brings came at about the same time I began running marathons. In my first few races, I quickly discovered that I was what is known as a "back-of-the-packer." As I pressed through each mile, often alone after most runners had finished and gone home, I was struck by how participating in a marathon (26.2 miles) mirrored what I was going through in my life. At that time, I was facing several personal setbacks, working through the grief of a divorce, making peace with failures, and trying to discern how to press on. Likewise, in the marathon I learned to run through pain, find training partners that fit my slow pace, push past "the wall" at about mile seventeen, patiently trudge through hours of loneliness and boredom, catch that coveted second wind, and then—finally—reach the goal and receive the reward. It turns out that every long run is a mini classroom.

I'll never forget a runner I met during my third marathon who taught me a lesson about passion. I'll call him Mick. Mick was seventy-five years old and had run more than a hundred marathons. I trotted up beside him about halfway through the race, and we struck up a conversation in which he told me he'd chipped his hip the previous summer and had had to take some time off running. He was just getting back on track. He had plans to do races the following two weekends in addition to the one we were running at the moment, he told me. Mick said he'd started running when he was fifty years old. He'd reevaluated his life at that point and decided that he needed to do something to ensure he wouldn't start sliding "downhill" as he'd watched his father do in midlife.

I was only forty at the time, but I had an epiphany that day running next to Mick: Passion is for now! Mick loved running. It made him feel alive and vibrant and real. Soon I picked up my pace and said goodbye to Mick (he was one of a very few runners slower than I was that day), but as I left him, I felt changed for the better with a new commitment. As I headed into my next decade, I was going to search out and engage in that which inspired my sense of passion. What was I waiting for?

What are you waiting for? Whether your passion is running, yoga, quilting, baking cakes, or playing soccer, let's make the most of this time in our lives. It's time to regroup, reevaluate, and run forward. Seek out that which makes you feel passionate and fully engaged.

"The most important thing is not the number of miles or the time it takes to finish a race or reach a goal. The reason to keep running is that out there is where I meet myself. Out there running is where I tell myself stories, where I cry spontaneously, where I am angry and happy, lost and found. As long as my legs work, I'll run."
—Cami Ostman from *Second Wind: One Woman's Midlife Quest to Run Seven Marathons on Seven Continents*

Putting It Into Practice

Intention Word: Passion

Reflection: What are your passions? What makes your heart flutter?

Running Mantra: Passion is for now!

Running Focus: Quick Feet. Instead of long strides, keep your feet under you and shuffle. Most people think that they need to lengthen their stride to run faster. The truth is, you get faster by how rapidly you bring your foot up and down off the ground. Concentrate on picking up your foot and quickly putting it back down. Think "Quick, Quick, Quick."

Week 1 Workouts

MONDAY

Benchmark Time-Trial: The benchmark is to determine what type of walking/running shape you are in right now. This information will be the baseline for all of your workouts, so please do this.

- 10 minutes slow walking or running warm-up

Time-Trial: 1-mile/1600 meters—4 times around the track or find a flat mile using your GPS—time yourself and write this time down

- 10 minutes slow walking or running cool-down

TUESDAY

- 2 miles slow, relaxed run

WEDNESDAY

Pacing Workout:

- 10 minutes slow walking or running warm-up
- 3 minutes at your current CH (Comfortably Hard/5K) pace alternating with 3 minutes slow running or walking
  — Repeat 4 times
- 10 minutes slow walking or running cool-down

THURSDAY

- 2 miles slow, relaxed run or cross training

FRIDAY

- Take this day off from working out or 2 miles slow

SATURDAY

Long Run:

- 2-mile run

SUNDAY

- Off

Nutrition Goal

This week, buy a nutritious food that you love and eat it. Do you love pine nuts but never buy them because they are so expensive? This week spend a little more on the healthy, nutritious food you love and less money on the less nutritious food and beverages that you habitually buy.

A New Beginning

When I (Cami) was in my twenties, I lived with an interesting conundrum. I was simultaneously terrified of the world around me (especially authority figures whom I assumed I needed to please in order to be safe and successful) and overly confident in making major life decisions. I read the faces of almost everyone in my life—parents, professors, ministers, and employers—in an attempt to gauge whether or not they were happy with my performance—and then changed my behavior based on what I suspected I read in their expressions. At the same time, I brazenly jumped into marriage at age twenty-three and made huge, life-altering demands of my (now ex) husband borne out of terrible insecurity and a ludicrous arrogance that I could make a marriage work properly by sheer force of will.

I know I'm not the only person who spent her twenties alternating between pandering to other people's perceived wishes and stomping her foot with ill-informed demands on others or the world. When my mid-thirties came along and brought with it a divorce and, eventually, a crisis of identity and faith, I was almost relieved. I was brought to my knees, exhausted from trying to control how others felt about me. I desperately needed to give myself permission to really evaluate who I had become and whether or not that person was someone I liked and wanted to continue being. I'd hit "the wall."

Have you hit your own wall in the marathon of life? If you have, you'll relate to the metaphor: It's that point (about seventeen to twenty miles into a literal marathon) when you feel like you've depleted your reserves and aren't quite sure how you'll get to the finish line, much less how you'll enjoy the journey.

Since the days when I hit my own wall and desperately sought to revise my life, I've worked as a therapist with hundreds of people who come to similar evaluative points in their lives. And one thing they all bring to the table when reexamining their life choices and the identities they've built for themselves is Bravery (if they don't bring it to the table right off the bat, often a crisis helps to develop it quickly). Yes, if you want to start a second act in your life, you'll need to be brave.

So, what is Bravery? And how do you know if you have enough of it to make a commitment to shed old, unhelpful values and behaviors, replacing them with new resolve and freedom to try new things? Here is my portrait of Bravery, as I have come to know her.

Bravery cries herself to sleep, but still wakes up in the morning, makes coffee, and dresses for work. She is resilient, knowing that what does not happen today may also not happen tomorrow, but it is important, and so she stays with it—unless she decides it's time to let it go (whatever "it" may be).

Bravery tells the truth—to herself and to others. She endures the disapproval of supervisors, and mentors, and she pushes away the needy tendrils of people who reach for her and hold on too tightly. She smiles when she is happy and weeps when she is sad, although her brothers and sisters don't care much for her authentic expressions of joy and grief.

Bravery takes chances, jumps out of planes, and learns to play the violin in her old age. But she does it all with intention, knowing (or knowing that she *will* know) what she hopes to gain. She considers her options and chooses this (or that) as consciously as she is able—and more consciously next time around when she has gained more insight.

Bravery winds her way through life's labyrinth with the bright light of audacity to show the way. She knows that she must be willing to meander amidst the unknown. She believes she has the right to explore dark corners, to make wrong turns, and to self-correct. She believes she is just as qualified to make brilliant discoveries as her brother, Heroism.

Bravery knows she is not alone in the world. When she falters, she reaches out to others. When she goes on an adventure, she leaves emergency numbers behind. She is accountable to others and others hold her accountable. They are invested in her success and she invests in theirs.

Bravery is tiny in her youth and takes only small, tentative steps, but as she practices her cadence and finds her perfect pace, she grows into a giantess. With time and experience, she expands into a commanding goddess who lifts others up and demands that they become brave, too.

If you see yourself reflected in this portrait of Bravery, you are already someone who has found her stride. If you'd like to see yourself in it, you're on the precipice of something revolutionary. Welcome to the journey to become ever more resilient, authentic, intentional, audacious, and accountable to living your best life.

Putting It Into Practice

Intention Word: Bravery

Reflection: When were you brave? How did you feel inside when you were brave? What did it feel like to take that first brave step?

Running Mantra: I am brave!

Running Focus: Keep your head aligned with your body. Keep your head up and facing forward. Sometimes during a race or a workout, we tend to put our head back or down to push through. This week, focus on keeping your neck and head straight, aligned, and relaxed.

Week 2 Workouts

MONDAY

Speed Workout:

- 10 minutes slow walking or running warm-up
- 30 seconds at your current 1-mile pace alternating with 1 minute slow running or walking repeated for 20 minutes
- 10 minutes slow walking or running cool-down

TUESDAY

- 2 miles slow, relaxed run

WEDNESDAY

Pacing Workout:

- 10 minutes slow walking or running warm-up
- 4 minutes at your current CH pace/3 minutes slow walk or jog
  — Repeat 4 times
- 10 minutes slow walking or running cool-down

THURSDAY

- 2 miles slow, relaxed run or cross training

FRIDAY

- Off or 2 miles slow, relaxed run

SATURDAY

Long Run:

- 3-mile run

SUNDAY

- Off

Nutrition Goal

This week, practice your bravery by stopping before you eat and asking yourself: Am I hungry? Is this food good for me? If your answer is no to either of these questions, set your timer for three minutes and do a different activity that feeds your soul (dance, read, meditate, pray, walk, lift hand weights, or just sit) before deciding whether and what to eat.

Love

While I love romantic love as much as the next gal, I also like to celebrate all of the loves of our lives. The older I get, the more I love the people, things, and creatures in my life with abandon. My dogs, my writing, the city where I make my home, the messy little condo I live in, and even the pouch of chub around my tummy all inspire my appreciation and, yes, affection.

If you're like me, it's easy to focus on the things around us or about ourselves that bug us. And don't get me wrong, I'm a huge fan of a good gripe session now and again. I don't see much value in burying our discouragement, frustration, or psychic pain because no one is served by denying our genuinely negative feelings. At the same time, I'm finding it more and more important to make an effort to notice how much there is to love about life.

Not long ago, I had breakfast with my maternal grandparents, ages eighty-five and eighty-seven. Grandma is in need of a hip replacement, and every move she makes right now sends shooting pain through her body. Grandpa is solicitous, patient, and as helpful to her as is possible, but he can't take her pain away. As I drove them to Denny's, parked directly in front of the building, and then helped Grandma out of my low-riding car, I reflected on how much I took my own agility for granted. I took a moment as I waited for her to right herself, closed my eyes, and thanked my body for how well it functioned at the moment.

Later that day, I learned that the Chuckanut 50K (a local thirty-one-mile race on mountainous trails) had opened up five hundred additional spots. I didn't have to think about it long. "Sign me up," I said. I guess I realize these days that I owe it to myself to grab opportunities that come my way. Life doesn't last forever. In fewer years than I've already lived, I'll be eighty-five years old (if I'm lucky), and I may need a hip replacement. If I do, it will be too late at that point to tick this 50K off my bucket list.

Remember the line in the Stephen Stills song about how if you can't have the person you love, you might as well love the person you're with? I've begun to feel that way about my body, my life, my dreams. I'm not all I imagined I would be when I was a young adult. Neither are you, but within this one life, just as it is, there are dreams to grab hold of, people to love and be loved by, and hidden gifts to distribute to your community. These exist side by side with grief, loss, illness, and devastation. I'm not saying life isn't hard, only that we each have the responsibility to notice what does give us joy.

Join me in loving what is right in front of us. And is there an opportunity that has been calling to you? A challenge you've always thought you might like to delve into? A pet at the shelter you'd like to rescue? A story you'd like to write? A recipe you'd like to try? *Carpe Diem*, my friends. Someday you may need a hip/knee/elbow/heart replacement. You may lose your sight or your hearing. I'm not trying to be alarmist, just realistic. Life doesn't last forever, but it will last through the day most likely. Love what you love with as much passion as you can muster! Be brave. Let's go!

Three of my favorite books on love: *Cold Sassy Tree* by Olive Ann Burns, *A Prayer for Owen Meany* by John Irving, and *Dogs Never Lie About Love* by Jeffrey Moussaieff Masson.

"The first thing is to love your sport. Never do it to please someone else. It has to be yours."
—Peggy Fleming

Putting It Into Practice

Intention Word: Love

Reflection: Look around you. What do you love? What do you love about yourself, others, your life, your job, your community?

Running Mantra: I have love in my life!

Running Focus: On the internet, watch a professional runner run. Study how she uses her arms and where her body is when her foot comes down on the ground. Practice using your arms like her, back and forth, aligned with your body.

Week 3 Workouts

MONDAY

Speed Workout:
- 10 minutes slow walking or running warm-up
- 1 minute at your current 1-mile pace alternating with 1 minute slow walk or jog repeated for 20 minutes
- 10 minutes slow walking or running cool-down

TUESDAY
- 2 miles slow, relaxed run

WEDNESDAY

Pacing Workout:
- 10 minutes slow walking or running warm-up
- 5 minutes at your current CH pace, alternating with 3 minutes slow running
  — Repeat 4 times
- 10 minutes slow walking or running cool-down

THURSDAY
- 2 miles slow, relaxed run or cross training

FRIDAY
- Off or 2 miles slow, relaxed run

SATURDAY

Long Run:

- 4-mile run

SUNDAY

- Off

Nutrition Goal

This week, try practicing mindful eating. Mindful eating allows us to appreciate the food that is replenishing our bodies. For one meal, sit down to eat and do nothing else (no TV, no phone, no talking to someone, no reading). Pay attention to what you are eating. Put your food, whatever it is (even if it's a highly caloric, less than perfect choice), on a nice plate, grab a cup of tea or coffee, sit down and REALLY enjoy it! When we slow down, appreciate, and enjoy something, the mental and physical results are always amazing.

"Me thinks that the moment my legs begin to move, my thoughts begin to flow."
—Henry David Thoreau

Training for Life

Any time we begin something new, especially if we don't get started until later in life, our first efforts can be clunky and unskilled. Remember the first time you went out for a run (or took up any other new endeavor)? I do. For my virgin run, I wore cotton sweats and a baggy t-shirt and felt sure that everyone who drove by me was sneering at how I was so obviously NOT a real runner.

I remember, too, my early days as an intern therapist. My first client was a woman who poured out her soul to me, really entrusting me with her troubled history and her heartbreak. As I listened to her trauma and her list of depressive symptoms, it was on the tip of my tongue to say, "You know, I think you should go see a therapist." I caught my advice before it came out. I was the therapist! Or at least I was pretending to be one at that point (thank goodness for supervision).

We often begin new roles or habits with a sense of being an imposter. But the more we practice, the more authentic we feel. For me, after years of running, I no longer feel like a bumbling pretender when I stand at a marathon starting line. And after many years in the counseling business, I no longer feel like a fake therapist when a client enters my office for an intake session.

What has led to my sense of mastery in both of these areas? Training and repetition! They can't be underestimated.

When you start running, for example, you begin by running from here to that telephone pole. When you get there, you walk until you catch your breath, and then you run to the next telephone pole. When you finish that first run, you're sore and tired, but the next day it's a little easier. Soon enough, you're up to a mile, then two, then ten—if you keep at it. One day you look around and realize you've turned yourself into runner.

It's the same process as you develop new boundaries or communication patterns. You'll be messy and awkward at first, but it'll get easier.

A dear friend of mine is trying to create boundaries with her sister. She wants to begin to make decisions on her own without the weight of her sister's opinions as the most pressing guiding factor in her mind. I encouraged her to remember that the first time she draws a line in the sand, it may be ugly—because she's unpracticed at it.

I also suggested she prepare her sister for her new resolve by having a conversation that goes something like this: "You know, sis, I'm trying to develop a sense of efficacy and strength for myself. As much as I love you, I need to start telling you when I'd rather not have your opinion. I'm going to try and be as gracious and kind as I can in my communication, but this is new for me, so I hope you'll forgive me when I do it messily. I hope you'll give me time to learn to create boundaries more smoothly."

What new patterns are you trying to create at this point in your life? Are you trying to speak your truth to important others? Are you adding vegetables to your diet? Asking your partner for what you need from him/her? Creating a schedule that allows for balance in your life? Or maybe you're training for a literal marathon.

Whatever you're training for, whatever new thing you're trying to implement:

1.   Keep doing it, even when your first many attempts are clunky.
2.   Tell those involved what you're up to so they can be prepared for the unfamiliar.
3.   Get support from neutral parties (friends, therapist, support group).

4. Forgive your own missteps and be patient with the process. Old habits die hard, but new habits feel great!

A terrific book on changing your habits: *Changing for Good* by Prochaska, Norcross, and DiClemente

Putting It Into Practice

Intention Word: Training/Repetition

Reflection: What healthy patterns do you want in your life? What is the first step that you need to take in "training" for health in your life?

Running Mantra: I am healthy and strong!

Running Focus: When running your workouts this week, make sure that your stride rate or cadence is between 160-180 spm (strides per minute). This means that your feet will touch the ground this many times per minute of running. The quicker you can get this spm during your faster workouts, the better not only for your speed, but also for the jarring on your body.

Week 4 Workouts

MONDAY

Speed Workout:
- 10 minutes slow walking or running warm-up
- 30 seconds at your current 1-mile pace/1 minute slow walk or jog
- 1 minute at your current 1-mile pace/1 minute slow walk or jog
- 90 seconds at your current 1-mile pace/1 minute slow walk or jog
- 2 minutes at your current 1-mile pace/1 minute slow walk or jog
- Repeat this sequence for a total of 20 minutes
- 10 minutes slow walking or running cool-down

TUESDAY
- 2 miles slow, relaxed run

WEDNESDAY

Pacing Workout:

- 10 minutes slow walking or running warm-up
- 6 minutes at your CH pace alternating with 3 minutes slow
  — Repeat 4 times
- 10 minutes slow walking or running cool-down

THURSDAY

- 2 miles slow, relaxed run or cross training

FRIDAY

- Off or 2 miles slow, relaxed run

SATURDAY

Long Run:

- 5 mile run

SUNDAY

Off

Nutrition Goal

This week, be aware of when and why you eat. We are all creatures of habit. We get out of bed, brush our teeth, drive to work, eat our meals, and even dress ourselves the same way each day. We also have certain foods we eat each day. Sometimes these foods or beverages are "linked" with certain times of day (like a coffee at noon), with other foods or beverages (like always having a donut with your coffee), or with an activity (like eating something salty while you watch TV). When we try to change these habits, we sometimes become uncomfortable and maybe even a little irritable. This discomfort will last a few days or until a new habit is formed. The hard part is getting through that first week or so of discomfort. But as speaker Michael Neill says, "You can do hard." Pay attention to your eating habits this week and make one small change to healthier living.

Why Does This Hurt So Much?

In adult life, transitions abound. We're sending children off to school, making arrangements for parents to be cared for, getting gray hair, and perhaps even grieving our way through a divorce or an illness. You wouldn't be alone if you asked yourself, "Why does this hurt so much?"

Change can be painful, and sorting through what is "normal" pain versus pain that may require you to seek help can be tricky. It never hurts to ask for extra support, but I've also learned that some pain does pass in its own time. It was the marathon that taught me this lesson.

My first marathon was almost a decade ago. The only reason I agreed to do it was because I was in love with a man who was a runner, and he'd invited me to join him in Prague—to run 26.2 miles. I was divorced, fighting depression, creeping toward forty, and I was a sometimes runner with an adventurous streak looking for a way to age more gracefully than I suspected I knew how to do. So, against the voice of reason whispering in my ear, I took on the hard work of training and decided to give the marathon a try.

I'm glad I did. The marathon was to become my great teacher, bringing all of my ideas as a therapist into finer focus over the next years, and that first foray into long distance running taught me something that no theory had ever been able to convey with quite the same clarity or poignancy:

When life hurts, you've got to dig deep and figure out if you should drop out of the race or keep pushing through.

The route that day of my first marathon in Prague was graced by warm sunshine and little breeze. I quite enjoyed the first many miles as we trotted through cobbled streets, past ancient buildings, across the Charles Bridge, and beside the Vltava River. As a back-of-the-packer, I felt no pressure or angst about racing. I was there purely for the experience, and because I'd trained up to about eighteen miles as I'd been advised, I'd almost chalked marathoning up as "easy," when I suddenly hit the wall at the twentieth mile.

A slow ache in my quadriceps that I had been successfully ignoring made itself known by cramping up—enough to hurt like hell but not enough to require an aid car. With tears running down my face, I turned to my friend, a seasoned marathoner, and told him, "I hurt."

He patted me on the shoulder and replied, "I know."

"No, I mean this hurts worse than anything I've ever felt before," I tried to clarify, thinking I hadn't conveyed the severity of the pain.

Now he looked over at me and waited until our gazes met. "That's how it's supposed to feel," he reiterated, sympathetically but firmly. "It'll go away in a couple of days." I struggled along beside him, stunned at the realization that pain this bad was a part of the marathon bargain. It was "normal" and didn't signal that I should stop running. Who knew?!

And isn't that how it is when we hit the wall in life? We come up against something that takes us off guard, or perhaps we've been doing something so long that we feel like we can't keep going. Pain is "normal" sometimes. It would be the rare person who doesn't hit that proverbial wall and hurt like crazy, especially in the midlife years, as one transition after another shakes our foundations. The trick is to figure out if what you're feeling is "normal," expected emotional pain related to where you are in the life-cycle or pain that might do you lasting harm or trauma. Here are a couple of things to ask yourself:

- Is the pain likely to go away on its own if you rest and take good care of yourself? If yes: rest and take care of yourself. If no: find someone to help you through it. Injury requires attention. There's no shame in stepping out of the race for a while to attend to your own healing.

- Is it a manageable ache or a shooting pain? Transitions can make you ache, but if even a normative transition (like launching your children into the world) feels like it's going to knock you down for good, why not find a "running partner" (therapist, coach, best friend, or doctor) who can trot alongside you and make the journey a little easier?

- When in your life have you felt this kind of pain before? When you know yourself well (after a few similar races), you'll know when getting aid is essential and when to simply press forward and wait out the ache. If in doubt, consult a fellow racer for another perspective.

We're all in this together.

"I have a principle for myself: I do not accept negativity. I've pushed the reset button and left past failures and disappointments behind. I simply refuse to look backwards. Self-acceptance and responsibility for my health are at the top of my list each and every day." —Rose Sporty Diva Coates

Putting It Into Practice

Intention Word: Persevere

Reflection: What is painful in your life right at this moment? If something is painful, where in your body do you feel that pain? If this pain had a color, what color would it be?

Running Mantra: I can persevere!

Running Focus: While running, pay attention to your breathing. Relax your breathing even when you are doing your speed workout. Accomplish this by expanding your stomach when you breathe in and making your stomach come in when breathing out. This is called belly breathing.

Week 5 Workouts

MONDAY

Speed Workout:

- 10 minutes slow walking or running warm-up
- 90 seconds at your current 1-mile pace/1 minute slow walk or jog
  — Repeat for 20 minutes
- 10 minutes slow walking or running cool-down

TUESDAY

- 2 miles slow, relaxed run

WEDNESDAY

Consistent Speed As Distance Increases Workout:

- 10 minutes slow walking or running warm-up

Ladder:

- 1 minute CH pace/2 minutes slow walk or jog walk or run
- 2 minutes CH pace/2 minutes slow walk or jog walk or run
- 3 minutes CH pace/2 minutes slow walk or jog walk or run
- 4 minutes CH pace/2 minutes slow walk or jog walk or run
- 3 minutes CH pace/2 minutes slow walk or jog walk or run
- 2 minutes CH pace/2 minutes slow walk or jog walk or run
- 1 minute CH pace/2 minutes slow walk or jog walk or run
- 10 minutes slow walking or running cool-down

THURSDAY

- 2 miles slow, relaxed run or cross training

FRIDAY

- Off or 2 miles slow, relaxed run

SATURDAY

Long Run:

- 6-mile run

SUNDAY

Off

Nutrition Goal

This week, pay attention to how different foods make you feel. After eating each meal, pay attention to how your stomach feels. How does your head feel? Do you feel sleepy or wide awake? Do you feel bloated or energized and ready to take on the world? By listening to your body, you'll discover the foods that will help you be at your best.

"Even if you haven't actually run, even if you're overweight, even if you were always the kid picked last in gym class, even if you're clumsy, even if you don't own a single piece of fitness equipment, you ARE a runner. You don't have to run fast to be a runner. You don't have to be skinny to be a runner. You don't have to run marathons to be a runner. You only have to want to run. Take your first step . . ."
—John "the penguin" Bingham, *No Need for Speed*

The Questions They Never Ask

Two years after my first book was published, there was a flurry of activity in my world as I quickly packed and bought tickets to New York City, where I was to be interviewed by Tim Gunn (of *Project Runway*) and Ty Pennington (of *Extreme Home Makeover*) on ABC's *The Revolution* about my personal revolution to turn myself from a depressed divorcee into a globe-trotting marathoner. Also on my trip to New York, I was able to meet (for the first time, face-to-face) and enjoy the company of my book agent, as well as spend a little time with old friends who lived in the area.

New York City is so grand and formidable that when I arrived on a Wednesday (as a first-time visitor), I instantly wondered what I'd gotten myself into, wondered if I would be able to navigate the subway system and find my way from point A to point B. Fortunately, when I arrived at the studio, the folks at *The Revolution* took me in hand and made me feel comfortable and safe with their hair and makeup artists and bustling producers making sure everyone was in the right place at the right time. By the time I actually shook hands with Tim and Ty, I was quite relaxed.

The gist of the interview explored how I used running and my seven-continent marathon quest to reenvision my life and my identity. Every word I said was true, but the interview was short and there was a lot left unsaid. In fact, I've done a number of interviews about *Second Wind* over the past years, and every interview seems to leave something important unexplored. After I left *The Revolution* studio, I got to thinking, "Why doesn't anyone ever ask?"

The questions no one has ever asked me, but which feel extremely relevant to my personal transformation, are about the deeper issues that emerged as I traveled the world. I'd love someone to ask: Who did you encounter that changed your way of thinking about culture/race/environmental preservation/politics? What made you laugh? What made you cry? What piece of art or natural wonder wowed you? When were you most afraid? When were you outraged? What/who/which place(s) did you fall in love with?

On and on I could go because, although I wrote more than three hundred pages about my 'round-the-world experience, there are thousands more unwritten. And I believe this is true for all of us—whether we are writers or not. Our most profound, paradigm-altering experiences often go unarticulated.

Here's an exercise: Write down the one question you wish someone would ask you. It could be that you wish your partner would ask you what makes you happy. Or maybe you'd like someone to ask you what the one gift is you'd like to leave for the world when you pass from it. Whatever it is, write it down. Then answer it. Take an afternoon to sit with tea and your journal. Answer that question until you've exhausted all you have to say. Explore every angle and facet. At the very least, we owe it to ourselves to ask the important questions, do we not?

"The marathon teaches a person to plan, to dream, to push through hard times, to admire unlikely people, to give up the penchant for perfectionism, and to accept life for the messy endeavor it is."
—Cami Ostman

Putting It Into Practice

Intention Word: Question

Reflection: What questions do you wish someone would ask you?

Running Mantra: I love _____ about myself!

Running Focus: During the "slow" parts of your workouts this week, really focus on bringing your heart rate down and relaxing. During the speed workouts and pacing/tempo aspects, work hard; it's important to keep your pace. So be sure to walk or run slowly in between the fast/pace sections of your workouts.

Week 6 Workouts

MONDAY
Speed Workout:
- 10 minutes slow walking or running warm-up
- 1 minute at your current 1-mile pace/1 minute slow walk or jog
- 90 seconds at your current 1-mile pace/1 minute slow walk or jog
- 2 minutes at your current 1-mile pace/1 minute slow walk or jog
  — Repeat this three-step sequence for a total of 20 minutes
- 10 minutes slow walking or running cool-down

TUESDAY
- 2 miles slow, relaxed run

WEDNESDAY
Pacing Workout:
- 10 minutes slow walking or running warm-up
- 7 minutes at your current CH pace alternating with 3 minutes slow
  — Repeat 3 times
- 10 minutes slow walking or running cool-down

THURSDAY
- 2 miles slow, relaxed run or cross training

FRIDAY
- Off or 2 miles slow, relaxed run

SATURDAY
Long Run:
- 7-mile run

SUNDAY

Off

Nutrition Goal

This week, try a new, healthy recipe. We often get into a routine of buying the same foods and making the same recipes. It's easy not to think too hard about what we're going to make for dinner, let alone try something different for breakfast. Take ten minutes this week to research a fun, healthy recipe, and write a shopping list around it. Enjoy planning, shopping for, and preparing a food that may become a new staple in your house.

"Take small, positive steps today for a healthier tomorrow."
—Carol Frazey

Progress

How do you know if you're making progress toward your goals?

When I run a long race, I rely heavily on mile markers. Since I'm such a slow-poke racer, there can be a full twelve minutes between each mile marker. Each time I see one up ahead in the distance, I let out a little relieved hoot. In some races, mile-markers are big and colorful—hard to miss, such as at the Tinkerbelle Half Marathon I ran last January where the numbers were flashed on large electronic placards and even heralded by Disney characters.

At more low-key races, mile-markers might be nothing more than a number written in black ink on an orange plastic traffic cone. You have to know what you're looking for to spot them.

But no matter the stature of the mile-marker, I give myself permission to engage in a bit of internal celebration each time I pass one. Why? Because the finish line is so far away from the starting line that if I waited until the end to celebrate, I would spend all my time on the course waiting to be triumphant rather than enjoying every step along the way. Certainly, the purpose of a goal is to reach the finish line, but if the journey isn't equally as (if not more) important, you might as well just drive over to the finish line and say, "Yep. There it is. I reached it."

No, what makes meeting a personal goal so life-changing is the distance between the beginning and the end—and achieving each benchmark along the way. Celebrating the benchmarks of completion adds to the joy and sense of accomplishment when you finally get to the finish. The feeling of exaltation gathers steam along the way.

What is the goal you're working toward nowadays? Are you writing a book? Planning a trip to Europe? Losing weight? Working on a degree? Training for a long race?

Great! Good for you for getting to the starting line. Be sure you identify your mile-markers. Every draft of every chapter written, every hotel reservation made, every pound lost, every test taken is a reason to let out a hoot and raise a glass to toast yourself.

Give this a try:

1. Write a goal you're shooting for at the bottom of a piece of paper.
2. At the top of the paper write today's date.
3. In between, identify ten benchmarks (ten steps or activities or achievements that indicate you're moving toward the goal).
4. Now, next to each benchmark, jot down a creative way to celebrate when you reach that mini-goal. Celebration can be as simple as calling a friend to announce your accomplishment or as complicated as buying yourself a whole new outfit. You get to decide.

What are you waiting for? Celebrate the benchmarks!

"[M]ake a radical change in your lifestyle and begin to boldly do things which you may previously never have thought of doing, or been too hesitant to attempt. So many people live within unhappy circumstances and yet will not take the initiative to change their situation because they are conditioned to a life of security, conformity, and conservation, all of which may appear to give one peace of mind, but in reality nothing is more damaging to the adventurous spirit within a [wo]man than a secure future. The very basic core of a [wo]man's living spirit is . . . [her] passion for adventure."
—Jon Krakauer, *Into the Wild*

Putting It Into Practice

Intention Word: Progress
Reflection: What is your goal? What are your mile-markers?
Running Mantra: I will reach my goal of _____!

Running Focus: Let's focus on your running head! What is going through your head while you run? Are you just trying to get through, having fun, playing a show tune, trying to catch another runner, telling yourself how slow you are, or planning your next vacation? When you are getting ready for a race, practice focusing on what you want to focus on during the race. If positive affirmations help you run faster, then focus on those which help you pick up your pace. If certain mantras or songs help you feel strong and fast, then use those during your training.

Week 7 Workouts

MONDAY
Speed Workout:
- 10 minutes slow walking or running warm-up
- 2 minutes at your current 1-mile pace/2 minutes slow walk or jog
  — Repeat for 20 minutes
- 10 minutes slow walking or running cool-down

TUESDAY
- 2 miles slow, relaxed run

WEDNESDAY
Tempo Workout:
- 10 minutes slow walking or running warm-up
- 15 minutes at your current CH pace
- 10 minutes slow walking or running cool-down

THURSDAY
- 2 miles slow, relaxed run or cross training

FRIDAY
- Off or 2 miles slow, relaxed run

SATURDAY
Long Run:
- 8-mile run

SUNDAY

Off

Nutrition Goal

This week, write down your main nutrition goal (Example: I will eat three fruits and four vegetables per day). Now, write down how you will mark reaching your goal for the day. Will you put a star on a calendar each day that you meet your goal and then post it on Facebook at the end of the month? What would motivate you to take this simple step each day?

"Running! If there's any activity happier, more exhilarating, more nourishing to the imagination, I can't think what it might be."
—Joyce Carol Oates, author

Changes!

August is my December, and September is my January. For the first three decades of my life, my stops and starts were dictated by the academic year—as a student, a teacher, and then a student again—and I've never gotten out of that groove. I've always thought of August as the time to assess how I'm doing on my goals and September as the time to start fresh and set new targets.

I know I'm not alone in ebbing and flowing with the cycles of the academic year. In August, many of us are coming to the end: of summer, of vacation, of reminiscing about our favorite moments with family. By September, we'll get back to work or school, hopefully with some renewed energy and resolve.

But how can you go about taking advantage of the opportunity for a fresh start? I always loved the Bible verse that states, "God's mercies are new every morning." What a wonderful sentiment that each day is a fresh opportunity—to shine, to live out loud, to pour ourselves into our passions and dreams, and to be committed to our values. As the one season (any season) comes to a close and the temperature in the air begins to feel differently on your skin, think about making a commitment to the following five actions:

1. Forgive yourself for past failures. "You can't go back in time" is a cliché precisely because it's true. Whatever you've done in the

past months (or years) that has taken you off course cannot be undone. Grieve your losses with all of your heart, but then let them go. Write them down on a piece of paper to be burned on your barbecue or buried in your backyard if you need to. Whatever you do to help yourself move on, recognize that the best way to "pay" for your mistakes is to learn the lessons they have to teach you and to go forward with new insight and wisdom.

2. Change your relationship with guilt and regret. This is related to what I said above, of course. Imagine Guilt as a large gorilla that has jumped on your back. You carry it around to remind yourself of what has gone wrong and that you shouldn't make the same mistakes again. The problem is that, since Guilt is so heavy, it prevents you from living into your best values and principles. Shuck it off your back, turn around, and point your finger at it and tell it to get lost.

3. Write down your values. If you know what you value and what you believe, you have a much better chance of aiming for the mark you'd like to hit, don't you think? As the next turn of season creeps up on us, why not take a minute to articulate what you value? Start the sentence with "I value . . ." or "I believe . . ." See what emerges. Once you've got it on paper, paste it on your bathroom mirror so you can read it as a mission statement every morning when you brush your teeth.

4. Develop a personal Bill of Rights. Many of us have never thought about our "non-negotiables," as I call them. What if you were sure you had the right to: Cry when you were sad? Leave the laundry undone? Talk about your feelings—out loud? Wear clothes that represent your personality? Read three hours a week? Take some time to write out a Bill of Rights for yourself. Write, "I have the right . . ." and make a list. Write down one "right" after the other. Don't stop until your mind is blank.

5. Know the benchmarks you'll celebrate. With all of the above done, you're ready to push the reset button on your goals and

dreams. Your last step is to decide what constitutes progress in the following months. How will you know that you're living into your values? How will you know that you're moving in the direction of your dreams? If I were a fly on the wall of your life, what would I see that would convince me you were making progress toward your goals? You have to know what progress looks like in order to know if you're making it. Set some small objectives for the next weeks and months. And decide how you'll celebrate when you reach those benchmarks.

The change of a season is the perfect time to restart and refresh your resolve. Take a deep breath and make a new commitment to yourself, your well-being, and your dreams. We are cheering for you!

"Running is the greatest metaphor for life, because you get out of it what you put into it."
—Oprah Winfrey

Putting It Into Practice:

Intention Word: Renew

Reflection: What steps can you take to feel renewed?

Running Mantra: I feel alive!

Running Focus: When you get to that "tired" point in your workout, practice driving your elbows back. To stay in balance, your legs must keep up with your arms. If you drive your elbows back, your arms go faster, and your legs must follow!

"You must do the thing you think you cannot do."
—Eleanor Roosevelt

Week 8 Workouts

MONDAY

Hill/Strength Workout:

- 10 minutes slow walking or running warm-up
- Find a gradual to steep hill to run up
- 30 seconds at your 1-mile pace up the hill/walk downhill
  — Repeat 10 times
- 10 minutes slow walking or running cool-down

TUESDAY

- 2 miles slow, relaxed run

WEDNESDAY

Consistent Speed As Distance Increases Workout:

- 10 minutes slow walking or running warm-up

Ladder:

- 1 minute CH pace/2 minutes slow walk or jog
- 2 minutes CH pace/2 minutes slow walk or jog
- 4 minutes CH pace/2 minutes slow walk or jog
- 6 minutes CH pace/2 minutes slow walk or jog
- 4 minutes CH pace/2 minutes slow walk or jog
- 2 minutes CH pace/2 minutes slow walk or jog
- 1 minute CH pace/2 minutes slow walk or jog
- 10 minutes slow walking or running cool-down

THURSDAY

- 2 miles slow walk or jog, relaxed run or cross training

FRIDAY

- Off or 2 miles slow, relaxed run

SATURDAY

Long Run:

- 9-mile run

SUNDAY

Off

"Running made me feel like a bird let out of a cage, I loved it that much."
—Priscilla Welch, Olympic Marathoner

Nutrition Goal

This week, keep a food diary for three days. By keeping a food diary for three days, you can find out the areas where you can improve your eating habits. For three days this week, write down when, what, and how much you eat. Knowing where you can improve in your diet is the first step in being the healthiest person you can be. Once you've kept track, examine your food diary, and make sure that you are getting the recommended amount of each nutrient. Look at your total calories for each day to determine if you are in energy balance.

"The secret of getting ahead is getting started. The secret to getting started is breaking your complex overwhelming tasks into small manageable tasks and then starting on the first one."
—Mark Twain

Seasons

Since I was in high school, my favorite poem has been one I learned about from Mr. Handby in my sophomore year. It goes like this:

Spring and Fall: to a Young Child
Margaret, are you grieving
Over Goldengrove unleaving?
Leaves, like the things of man, you
With your fresh thoughts care for, can you?
Ah! as the heart grows older
It will come to such sights colder
By and by, nor spare a sigh
Though worlds of wanwood leafmeal lie;
And yet you will weep and know why.
Now no matter, child, the name:
Sorrow's springs are the same.
Nor mouth had, no nor mind, expressed
What heart heard of, ghost guessed:
It is the blight man was born for,
It is Margaret you mourn for.

—Gerard Manley Hopkins (1844-1889)

Whenever the leaves turn color and then drop from the trees, I admit that I annually feel sad—just like the Margaret of Hopkins' poem. I start to feel blue that the days will grow shorter and that life, itself, is short. I feel melancholy about my previous year's New Year's goals. If I've met them, the journey is over; if I haven't met them, I feel less than successful.

And then, each fall, there comes a day when I look around and all of the trees are bare. They look dead and brittle. And this makes me mad. Why do they have to go naked for six months? And why do I have to look out my window and see gray: gray sky and gray sticks poking up from bare trees? It isn't fair!

But usually around the end of December, I remember that a new year is about to begin. The hope for a new beginning, the coveted "second wind," is what gets me through the dark days of dropping leaves and cloudy skies.

I don't know about you, but the end of every project (for me right now it's completing an anthology; for you it may be the end of your child-rearing, or leaving a job, or the dissolution of a marriage) ignites this same sad to mad to hope-for-the-future cycle.

When you've finished one thing but don't yet have direction or inclination to start another, there is a winter in your heart. If you're having winter in your life, consider letting it be. What if you don't judge yourself for sadness and anger or for that bittersweet sense of nostalgia that sometimes overcomes us when we get the first hard rains of the season? What if you just let yourself be where you are, wandering through the dropping leaves and then, when it's time, reaching up to touch a crisp, cold, empty branch, until a new energy wells up inside? What if you/we/I go ahead and trust that the warm winds of spring will come one day, and there's nothing to do to hurry it along? Breathe. Breathe into the season.

"That's the thing about running: your greatest runs are rarely measured by racing success. They are moments in time when running allows you to see how wonderful your life is."
—Kara Goucher, 2008 Olympian in the 10K

Putting It Into Practice

Intention Word: Rest

Reflection: What part of your life is going from Autumn to Winter? What are you looking forward to?

Running Mantra: I am in the moment!

Running Focus: Are you ready for the changing of seasons? What are you going to put into place to help yourself stay consistent in the months ahead? Do you have comfortable clothing? Here are some ideas to help you stay comfortable and dry in the weeks ahead.

Choosing running clothing can be expensive and confusing. Here are a few basics to help take the guesswork out of what to wear:

Clothing Materials: To keep you cool and dry, here are a few thoughts about what to look for when buying running clothes. Just Say No to Cotton—the word "cotton" should not be in the materials list. Cotton absorbs perspiration. This can cause chaffing, blisters, and make you feel uncomfortable.

Words to look for: Poly or Polyester, Nylon, Wicking, Breathable, Drymax, Spandex, Lycra®, Dri-FIT®, COOLMESH®

Running Basics:

- Running shoes
- Running bra
- Socks
- Shorts, tights, or capris
- Running shirt

Extras:

- Hat
- Running underwear
- Water bottle holder (belt or handheld)

Shop local when you can, but here are a few national stores to find great running gear:

- Sierra Trading Post www.sierratradingpost.com
- Campmor www.campmor.com

- REI Outlet www.rei.com/outlet
- T.J. Maxx, Marshalls, and Ross stores

Week 9 Workouts

MONDAY

Speed Workout:

- 10 minutes slow walking or running warm-up
- 30 seconds at your current 1-mile pace/1 minute slow walk or jog
- 1 minute at your current 1-mile pace/1 minute slow walk or jog
- 90 seconds at your current 1-mile pace/1 minute slow walk or jog
- 2 minutes at your current 1-mile pace/ 1 minute slow walk or jog
  — Repeat this four-step sequence for a total of 25 minutes
- 10 minutes slow walking or running cool-down

TUESDAY

- 2 miles slow, relaxed run

WEDNESDAY

Pacing Workout:

- 10 minutes slow walking or running warm-up
- 8 minutes at your current CH pace/4 minutes slow
  — Repeat 3 times
- 10 minutes slow walking or running cool-down

THURSDAY

- 3 miles slow, relaxed run or cross training

FRIDAY

- Off or 2 miles slow, relaxed run

SATURDAY

Long Run:

- 10-mile run

SUNDAY

Off

Nutrition Goal

This week, make a comfort food meal and allow yourself to truly enjoy it. It seems like nowadays we are constantly counting calories, weighing themselves, and talking about what we shouldn't have eaten. What if we just allowed ourselves to eat something without guilt, without shame, without remorse? If we do this one simple act of eating a comfort meal consciously and without guilt, we will be more conscientious of our eating in general and more aware of how and why we eat.

Self-Soothing or Self-Medication

I've heard a lot of runners say things like, "Running is my therapy," or "Running keeps me sane." I've even heard, "Running is my drug." When my partner gets home at the end of the day, he often tells me he needs to get out on the trails to "clear the cobwebs" from his mind—like a mind dump. He likes to leave his work-related stress out in the woods.

I understand these sentiments and echo them, but for me running is even more than my therapy or a way to clear cobwebs. Without a doubt, it is my center, my anchor, and my antidepressant. Some may call it self-medicating (because it is addicting), but I call it legitimate, healthy self-soothing. Whatever you call it, running works.

I come from a family in which depression has been a troubling feature for as long as I can remember, and some family members have heavily self-medicated with alcohol until their addictions led to so many health and relational problems that they were forced to make the decision to get help and stop drinking. As for me, I had my own first major depressive episode when I was twenty-seven; it scared the hell out of me.

I knew drinking wasn't a good solution to what could be a long relationship with depression, but I didn't know what to do instead. Over the many years since then, I've done a number of things to manage depression. Now, in midlife, I know which of my efforts really work—and many of them have. For example, I got myself a dog (now I have two); I went to therapy; I took a low dose of an SSRI that kept some of the worst negative thoughts in check; and I surrounded myself with people who love me and are caring toward me during my tough moments. But nothing has been as powerful a weapon against the darkness of depression as the hard-pounding, repetitive movement of running.

Ever since I discovered this for myself, I've encouraged my clients and friends (and anyone else who will listen) to find an activity that has some of the same qualities as running to help soothe their troubled psychological edges. And while I understand that running isn't for everyone, anyone can look at the gains running has to offer and find those gains in other activities more suited to individual preferences. What is it about running that leads to a lifting of depressive symptoms? Here are a few thoughts:

- You can get lost in running and temporarily move your focus away from old, circular, catastrophic thoughts.
- It requires a shift in attention from the internal emotional life to the external physical world (if you don't make this shift, you'll run into things—literally).
- It invites you to press through uncomfortable feelings like boredom, irritation, or the temptation to quit.
- It makes you legitimately tired—in that healthy way you should be tired when you've exerted yourself.
- It gives you a sense of accomplishment when you're done.

The Mayo clinic says that hard exercise can actually release mood stabilizing chemicals in the brain, boost your immune system, and increase body temperature which may have a "calming effect." And while I favor hard exercise as my depression-fighting superpower, there are many kinds of activities that can offer the same sorts of results (yoga, meditation, dancing, playing the piano, just to name a few). If you're tempted to self-medicate with something that will not ultimately add value to your life (like alcohol or numbing out in front of the TV), at least take a few moments and ask yourself what you could do instead that might evoke the responses listed above. (And, of course, always ask for help from your doc and/or therapist when dealing with major depression.)

Midlife can be a difficult time for many of us. There are a multitude of transitions on the horizon. Just this week, I've had two friends and one client tell me that they feel life changes coming their way, and the melancholy is setting in as they wonder where they'll get the energy to manage them. My response? Why not proactively look for some healthy ways to self-soothe? It's worth a try.

Putting It Into Practice

Intention Word: Health
Reflection: What are your current addictions? What healthy habits could replace them?
Running Mantra: I choose health!
Running Focus: One way to push your way uphill while running is to drop your head slightly and just focus on small, quick steps. Think of your feet like popcorn. Quick pop up and quickly back down for the footfall.

Week 10 Workouts

MONDAY

Hill/Strength Workout:

- 10 minutes slow walking or running warm-up
- Find a gradual-to-steep hill to run up
- 1 minute at your 1-mile pace uphill/walk downhill
  — Repeat 10 times
- 10 minutes slow walking or running cool-down

TUESDAY

- 3 miles slow, relaxed run

WEDNESDAY

Tempo Workout:

- 10 minutes slow walking or running warm-up
- 17 minutes at your current CH pace
- 10 minutes slow walking or running cool-down

THURSDAY

- 3 miles slow, relaxed run or cross training

FRIDAY

- Off or 2 miles slow, relaxed run

SATURDAY

Long Run:

- 7-mile run

SUNDAY

Off

Nutrition Goal

Eat a healthy breakfast every day. According to the American Heart Association, people who eat breakfast daily are less likely to be obese, have diabetes, or have heart disease. A healthy breakfast can include a variety of foods. Because of the popularization of high-protein diets, people have been led to believe that foods such as bacon and sausage can constitute a healthy breakfast. While these foods may make someone feel full, the saturated fat in these foods is linked to heart disease, which is a number-one killer of Americans. Prepackaged whole-grain cereals can be a fast, convenient, healthy breakfast food. Look for cereals that list whole grain or bran as the first ingredient and contain at least two grams of fiber. The more fiber it contains, the better it is for you.

The First Step in Moving Forward is Self-Forgiveness

Setting goals is essential for healthy living. We know that people who set goals are more focused and happier; they move through life with a sense of purpose. From a "narrative therapy" perspective, reaching a goal you've set can give you evidence that the positive, preferred meanings you make about your life are valid.

But have you ever set a goal for yourself and then failed to live up to or reach it? Of course you have, if you're human. Everyone has set out on a journey, literal or metaphorical, and failed to get to their intended destination. I recently worked with a therapy client who made her way through a graduate program, and then, with only a few weeks remaining before graduation, had an epiphany that she'd taken the wrong course of study. She dropped out suddenly, and while she never doubted her decision to change directions, she simply could not forgive herself for what she perceived as a grievous failure to complete what she'd started.

A few weeks ago, I experienced my own failure to reach a goal. I participated in a marathon I thought would be one of my best. Always a back-of-the-packer, my running goals tend to be modest, but after scrutinizing the elevation chart for the course, I felt sure I could get my best finish time in what would be my twentieth race of the marathon distance or longer. I was in good shape, and I felt my training had been adequate. The course provided a net loss of elevation, and since I'm a stable downhill runner, I decided to set my goal for a sub five-hour marathon—something I've only ever achieved once before.

On Sunday morning when the race got going, however, a number of things went wrong. I started too fast and cramped up by mile sixteen. This took me down to slower than my usual pace as I struggled with pain that ran from my toes to my nose. Rather than taking some deep breaths and re-evaluating my goal (maybe setting a new one that was more achievable, given the circumstances), I let disappointment and self-recrimination get the best of me. For the better part of the ten remaining miles, I vacillated between fighting back tears and giving in to them.

When I finally crossed the finish line, a snotty, puffy-eyed mess, I had not only NOT achieved my best marathon time, I had achieved one of my worst.

"Well, at least you crossed the line," you say. Sure. I'll give you that. But just like you, I struggle with my own version of self-reproach on my bad days, and I wasn't quick to let myself off the hook for failing to run a smart race. It was only after a good meal, a shower, and a very long, deep sleep that I came to my senses and remembered how I believe that very few failures in this life (if any) should preclude self-forgiveness.

To quote a fellow runner friend: "Setting goals is a good thing. Being defined by them is probably not such a good idea." That's right! Failing to see something through the way we originally envisioned it does not have to define who we are.

What race are you running? And what are the failures, big or small, you're ruminating over? Did you reach the destination, but in such poor condition that you vowed never to get into another similar situation again? Perhaps you're notoriously hard on yourself, and no matter what you achieve, it's never enough.

If there's one thing running has taught me, it's that there is always another chance. If you're facing a failure, great or small, first forgive yourself. Take some time to get into a mental space where you can quiet your inner critic. Whether you tried your hardest to plan for success, as I did on my recent race, or slacked off and failed to adequately throw yourself into the project/relationship/job, it's too late to go back in time. So stop doing that. You'll never be any younger than you are today (never get to do your first marriage or raise your children over again), but you can look ahead. After you've let go of what haunts you (easier said than done, I know; don't be afraid to seek help), take some time to understand what went wrong and to imagine how you would do things differently next time. Then, when you're ready, look for another race. This time, you'll know yourself better than the last time. This time, it also won't be perfect and you may not achieve exactly what you're hoping for. This is the cycle of life. And in life, as in running, forgiving oneself makes it possible to move forward after failure—over and over again.

Putting It Into Practice

Intention Word: Forgive
Reflection: Are you ready to forgive yourself?
Running Mantra: I forgive myself!
Running Focus: To help you stay strong and injury-free, add stretching to your regular running routine. MayoClinic.com has photos to show you how to stretch correctly.

Week 11 Workouts

MONDAY
Speed Workout:
- 10 minutes slow walking or running warm-up
- 30 seconds at your current 1-mile pace/1 minute slow
  — Repeat for 25 minutes
- 10 minutes slow walking or running cool-down

TUESDAY
- 3 miles slow, relaxed run

WEDNESDAY

Consistent Speed As Distance Increases Workout:

- 10 minutes slow walking or running warm-up

Ladder:

- 1 minute CH pace/1 minute slow walk or jog
- 2 minutes CH pace/1 minute slow walk or jog
- 3 minutes CH pace/1 minute slow walk or jog
- 4 minutes CH pace/1 minute slow walk or jog
- 3 minutes CH pace/1 minute slow walk or jog
- 2 minutes CH pace/1 minute slow walk or jog
- 1 minute CH pace/1 minute slow walk or jog
- 10 minutes slow walking or running cool-down

THURSDAY

- 3 miles slow, relaxed run or cross training

FRIDAY

- Off or 2 miles slow, relaxed run

SATURDAY

Long Run:

- 11-mile run

SUNDAY

Off

Nutrition Goal

This week, add one more serving of vegetables to your diet each day. When most people think of losing weight, they think of what they need to take out of their diet. Stay away from sugar, salt, too much fat, for example. But instead, we can decide what we will add to our diet each day.

Health statistics show that we should add more vegetables to our diet to stay healthy. So let's do it. Most vegetables are low in calories and high in vitamins, minerals, and fiber. Choose a veggie, and bring it on board!

What to Do When a Heavy Heart Puts You on the Couch

What do you do when a heavy heart puts you on the couch?

Do you feel stuck in a self-definition that isn't quite working for you at the moment? Maybe you've been pegged by loved ones or co-workers in a way that doesn't feel fair or true (you've been blamed or labeled). Perhaps you've had a conflict with someone and your heart hurts so much you can't get a deep breath. You may have suffered a loss that makes you sadder than you would have expected. Whatever it is, it has flattened you and put you on the couch for the time being. If we were to be honest with one another, we could all speak of many times like this in our lives.

We sometimes get into mental holding patterns that create pain, fear, or anger, but most of us also have ways of working through tough, hardened states of mind so we can get unstuck and get back to whatever is normal and healthy in our lives. When I feel exceedingly blue, anxious, angry, or confused, I take a run. Years ago, I discovered that moving my body was the key to loosening up my psychic knots. I also discovered a paradox to this course of action. When I'm in a heavy state of mind, I tend to lack the energy to get myself out on the trail. Doing what I know is good for me is often an act of will that takes a firm decision and then a leap of faith (that it will actually make me feel better), but once I've gotten off the sofa and out the door, my inner world opens up and my constricted thinking often gives way to a more spacious perspective.

You know what I'm talking about, I'm sure. The "key" to your well-being may not be running; instead, it may be meditation, prayer, or a warm bath. It could well be escaping into a good book or cranking up the volume of your music and dancing behind closed doors. But whatever it is, you know that when you do it, your heavy state of mind will begin to lift and whatever you're wrestling with will start to untangle itself and loosen its tendrils ever-so-slightly. You also know what I mean when I say it takes an act of will to engage in the activity that will give you relief. Energy you don't exactly have in the dark, heavy moments is exactly what is required to produce relief, right?

If you're on the couch right now, struggling to take the step you need in order to lift the heaviness, consider what I do to get myself out the door and onto the trail during hard times:

1. Suit up. I put my running clothes on as a first step—even before committing to heading outside. For you, go ahead and set yourself up for your chosen course of action. Dig out your favorite music; organize your yarn and knitting needles; pull your meditation cushion out of the closet. Make available for yourself whatever accoutrements you need for the self-care activity that will help you lift away the weightiness of your emotional state.

2. Call your running partner. I call my neighbor, Julie, who almost always agrees to go running with me. Who will hold *you* accountable to be good to yourself? Will your best friend go to a concert with you? Will your meditation teacher (or your AA sponsor) come over and sit with you? If you don't have a "running partner," you may want to consider finding a therapist or coach to partner with until you build a community that will invest in your well-being.

3. One, two, three—out the door. But slowly. On sad, hard days I start by walking and work my way up to a run. Be gentle with your heavy-hearted self. Maybe you only have the oomph to read a few passages out of your Holy Book or one chapter from your escapist novel. Perhaps you can't stay more than five minutes in your

bubble bath before you're ready for bed. It's okay. The very act of doing one self-loving thing provides encouragement to do more of it tomorrow. One slow mile today, and by the end of the week (or the month, if this is a persistent heaviness), you'll be back up to your 5K pace.

Putting It Into Practice

Intention Word: Small Step
Reflection: What is one small step that you can make today toward health?
Running Mantra: I can!
Running Focus: Practice quick steps again this week. This time, focus on bringing your foot down quickly, yet gently. Again, say to yourself, "Quick. Quick. Quick."

Week 12 Workouts

MONDAY

Benchmark Time-Trial Revisited
- 10 minutes slow walking or running warm-up

Time-Trial:
- 1-mile/1600 meters—4 times around the track. Time yourself and write this time down. Has it changed?
- 10 minutes slow walking or running cool-down

TUESDAY
- 3 miles slow, relaxed run

WEDNESDAY

Pacing Workout:
- 10 minutes slow walking or running warm-up
- 9 minutes at your new CH pace/4 minutes slow
  — Repeat 2 times
- 10 minutes slow walking or running cool-down

THURSDAY

- 3 miles slow, relaxed run or cross training

FRIDAY

- Off or 2 miles slow, relaxed run

SATURDAY

Long Run:

- 8-mile run

SUNDAY

Off

Nutrition Goal

This week, look at or think about your reasons for living a healthy lifestyle before eating. Having a purpose helps us make better choices. If we know where we are going, we are more likely to make choices that will help us move in that direction. Knowing the personal reasons why you want to make healthful food choices makes a few seconds of taste bud ecstasy just not worth the time!

Together AND Alone: A Paradox

At the beginning of my second marriage, I had a profound revelation. It came to me during a soaking Northwest rainstorm on a June morning. My new husband and I had driven into Canada to participate in a half marathon in the beautiful city of Vancouver. Because we were newlyweds (and in spite of the fact that we'd both experienced a great deal of disillusionment through our respective divorces), my beloved and I were idealistic and determined to forge a life of harmonic tranquility. And to that end, we'd concocted a plan to run marathons together—all around the world. Hand in hand, we believed we would take on the marathon of life, keeping pace with each other peacefully and cohesively.

But that dreary, drizzling morning, I was about to become disenchanted with our ideal and at the same time learn a principle that has served me very well in all my longstanding relationships. As the starting gun sounded and we began the first mile of the course, the rain, which had been beating down since we'd left our home two hours earlier, pounded impossibly harder. It came upon us with resolve, and the wind blew steadier with each passing minute, until we were being pelted with a sideways stream of relentless cold and wet.

We tried to buck up and keep a good attitude (at least I did) as we forged forward one soggy step at a time, but the chillier and more drenched we became, the harder it was to stay happy. My new husband, chilled to the bone, began to feel a reasonable urgency to pick up his pace and finish the race as quickly as possible. Unfortunately, being smaller and less athletic, I could go no faster. I struggled beside him as he became disgruntled and I felt ever more inadequate.

I shall only relate that a nasty argument ensued, the maddening details of which I shall spare the reader. But suffice it to say that by the end of the 13.1 miles, this runner was seriously questioning the bliss of her new relationship. I was soaked and sad as we crossed the finish line, even though, true to our promise to each other, we were together as we puttered through the final yards of the race.

On the drive home, I struggled with my troubled thoughts, despairing of our ability to jog through life in tandem. Then, I had my epiphany. We shouldn't do it! We were not meant to run together. We were different kinds of runners with vastly different paces and goals. Furthermore, running separately would not only NOT ruin our relationship, it would improve it. We could participate in running events alone and meet up at the end to swap stories. This way, I could go at my own slow pace without apologizing for who I was, and he could race comfortably and feel he was doing his best. My new husband agreed. This was a better plan.

So often, we insist others must be like us—fully be "with" us—in order to experience connection and solidarity. But this is nonsense, isn't it? Especially as we navigate life's major transitions and find ourselves evaluating how we've done so far at living out our authentic dreams and values, there can be a great freedom in realizing we've got enough drive, fortitude, patience, or grace to go it alone (whatever "it" is for you). You can certainly appreciate support from your loved ones for both your grief and your victories, but the internal journey is yours alone. No one else is in there with you, after all. Just as no one else can complete a race for me, no one but you can fully/totally/absolutely share your internal life. This can be a sad but liberating realization!

Somehow, embracing the paradox I call "living together AND alone" frees us from seeking approval and then being shattered when it isn't perfectly forthcoming. Instead of looking for approval and enmeshment, we can learn respect for differences and experience healthy autonomy (I'm not saying it's easy, just important).

What is looming ahead for you? Is it seeing your child off to college? Is it a new job? A divorce? A diagnosis that scares the hell out of you? If you knew you could do it your own messy (or slow) way without apologizing for your inadequacies and still connect with important others for support, encouragement, and even deep understanding, would that free you up to move forward with more abandon? Would it give you permission to find your own groove while still admiring someone else's way of being or doing? Just something to think about.

Putting It Into Practice

Intention Word: Authenticity
Reflection: What is real and true for you? What do you really want to do?
Running Mantra: I have the right to be myself!
Running Focus: As you run, pay attention to how your shoulders feel. As you get tired, do they tense up? Practice keeping your shoulders loose by shaking them out, making a big windmill with your arms, and running with totally relaxed, jelly arms. This may look funny, but it will help remind you to loosen your shoulders, and therefore, have a more efficient stride.

Week 13 Workouts

MONDAY

Speed Workout:
- 10 minutes slow walking or running warm-up
- 30 seconds at your current 1-mile pace/1 minute slow walk or jog
- 1 minute at your current 1-mile pace/1 minute slow walk or jog
- 90 seconds at your current 1-mile pace/1 minute slow walk or jog
- 2 minutes at your current 1-mile pace/ 1 minute slow walk or jog
  — Repeat this four-step sequence for a total of 25 minutes
- 10 minutes slow walking or running cool-down

TUESDAY
- 3 miles slow, relaxed run

WEDNESDAY
Tempo Workout:
- 10 minutes slow walking or running warm-up
- 20 minutes at your current CH pace
- 10 minutes slow walking or running cool-down

THURSDAY
- 4 miles slow, relaxed run or cross training

FRIDAY
- Off or 2 miles slow, relaxed run

SATURDAY
Long Run:
- 12-mile run

SUNDAY
Off

Nutrition Goal

This week, make a shopping list of all of your favorite healthy foods. We are constantly bombarded by messages of what we should be eating, what we shouldn't be eating, and what everyone else is eating. Who cares? What do you want to eat? Do you know that you can lose weight eating only French fries, chocolate cookies, and donuts? Yes, if you burn more calories moving and exercising than you take in from these foods, you will lose weight. While I don't recommend this diet, it is possible. Instead, I advocate making healthy food choices, and NOT total deprivation. Take some time this week to build your own, individual shopping list. Include healthy choices, of course, but don't be afraid to include a few things you "shouldn't" eat. Just be sure to eat those items mindfully and in moderation.

Navigating the Ultras in Life

I recently took part in an "ultra" marathon. While marathons are always 26.2 miles, ultras are races of any distance longer than this (the Leadville Trail Race in Colorado, for example, is 100 miles). They're usually raced on trails, often over mountains in isolated areas. And because the terrain they cover can be uneven and peppered with impediments such as rocks and roots, running them is more technical and runners must be comfortable with rugged conditions. This means the crowd that takes part in ultra-races are more the flannel-sporting, beanie-wearing sort and less the match-your-running-shoes-with-your-sparkly-headband kind. (I enjoy both kinds of runners, by the way, and keep both sparkles and flannel in my closet.) The ultra-race I participated in last weekend was a 50-kilometer (or 31-mile) grunt through woods, up mountain trails, in the mud, with rain, snow, and hail beating down from above. I was on my feet for over nine hours (more than twice as long as the winner of the race), and mine is the last recorded finish time—but I did finish.

After several days of recovery, I tried to mine the metaphors from my running experiences because running has become my best teacher, my most faithful source of consistent wisdom, but what kept coming to me was: "Dang, that was hard!" And then it occurred to me: That sentiment IS the metaphor I must integrate into the rest of my life.

Let's face it, we all have "ultras" in our lives. You have four children, for example. Three of them are regular, run-of-the-mill marathons (you put in long, hard hours and even navigate big hills along the way, but it's doable even if it's slow going sometimes), and then you've got one ultra-kid, the rearing and raising of whom is much more mountainous, rugged, and messy. You've got to spend money on special equipment, stop for long periods at the aid stations to regroup, and get comfortable never knowing what's around the next switchback.

Marriage, I think, is an ultra-relationship. Friendships can get hairy and take a great amount of effort and commitment to maintain (especially the lifelong kind), but there's nothing like marital partnership to test your mettle. I was talking on the phone the other day with a non-runner friend who's worked hard on her marriage for twenty years—reading books on communication and attending marriage counseling consistently. She said, "My marriage is my ultra-marathon. I've made the commitment to stay in this race until the finish line, no matter how many rainstorms I face." Mind you, plenty of runners in a race as hard as an ultra-marathon make the choice to drop out. People get hurt barreling down steep, rocky trails covered in mud. As always, you need to know when taking a DNF (Did Not Finish) is the wisest, healthiest decision. If you don't stop to assess what to do when you're hurt (in a race or in a marriage), you may risk permanent damage.

And what about serious illness? Isn't living with illness "ultra-living" at its most difficult? When you're fighting for your very survival, alone inside a body that isn't healing itself or is chronically aching, you have to tolerate extended periods of terrible discomfort, often only hoping for a favorable finish line out there beyond the forest.

So what does it take to live in the "ultras" of life? How do we keep going when the road seems impossibly long and impassible? I have a few thoughts, fresh on my mind, as it turns out.

- **Practice Mindfulness**: Mindfulness is a popular idea these days and for good reason. It's about living in the moment—this very moment—without fretting over what's ahead or ruminating about what's in the past. Mindfulness invites us to focus on taking just this one stride—on stepping safely—and landing on solid ground.

In Alcoholics Anonymous, they call it making a decision to do "the next right thing." And since we can't see how long the twisting, gnarly trail is from here, all we can do is to take the next clear step. My favorite book on mindfulness these days is Tara Brach's *Radical Acceptance*.

- **Stay Fueled**: In order to maintain the kind of resilience an ultra requires, you've got to stay properly fueled. Know what nourishes you and prepare to have plenty of it with you on the journey. What revives, heals, and nurtures you? What makes you feel filled up and renewed? If you're in a long, grueling race, make sure you prepare every morning to have enough fuel (time with loved ones, fresh air, moments alone with your cat on your lap—whatever it takes). Nobody can keep going without taking in plenty of that which allows them to put energy out. And don't be afraid to take "walk breaks" often to restore your energy.

- **Be Gentle with Your Self-Talk**: In an ultra, you're bound to stumble over obstacles—maybe you'll even fall. When this happens, you'll get up, take a few moments to recover (maybe have a good cry), and then move forward again. Unfortunately, we sometimes get so mean with ourselves when we stumble, and meanness saps away precious energy we need if we're to keep going. Instead of saying to yourself, "How stupid!" when you make a misstep, try, "It's OK, honey. I'll help you get your balance back." How much anxiety would be lifted? How much calm would result? Encouragement is a powerful energizer and something we can do for ourselves as well as for others.

- **Assemble a Team**: Ultra experiences shouldn't be embarked on alone. Who can come alongside you for even a five-mile stretch? Is there someone who can meet you every few miles to make sure you're refueling? It's crucial to have a team of a few people who see what you're doing, appreciate your struggle, and want to support you as you navigate the worst of the terrain. Who are these people for you? Maybe they include professionals who have helped others navigate such situations. Whoever they are, don't be afraid to call on them—often, if necessary.

Be brave, dear ultra-runner. Move through your situation stride by stride. And don't forget to breathe.

"Running has given me the courage to start, the determination to keep trying, and the childlike spirit to have fun along the way. Run often and run long, but never outrun your joy of running."
—Julie Isphording, former Olympian who ran the first-ever women's Olympic Marathon in 1984 in Los Angeles

Putting It Into Practice

Intention Word: Now

Reflection: How do you practice mindfulness in your life?

Running Mantra: One step at a time!

Running Focus: Having a strong core is essential to staying healthy and strong your entire life. This week, add the Three-Minute Core Workout to your exercise routine. You can do anything for three minutes! Rest as you need to during each 1-minute exercise, then get back to it. Here is the workout:

- 1 Minute of Plank
- 1 Minute of Crunches
- 1 Minute of Push-ups

Week 14 Workouts

MONDAY

Hill/Strength Workout:

- 10 minutes slow walking or running warm-up
- Find a gradual to steep hill to run up
- 2 minutes at your current 1-mile pace uphill/walk downhill
  — Repeat 6 times
- 10 minutes slow walking or running cool-down

TUESDAY

- 4 miles slow, relaxed run

WEDNESDAY

Consistent Speed as Distance Increases Workout:

- 10 minutes slow walking or running warm-up

Ladder:

- 1 minute at CH pace/1 minute slow walk or jog
- 2 minutes CH pace/1 minute slow walk or jog
- 4 minutes CH pace/1 minute slow walk or jog
- 6 minutes CH pace/1 minute slow walk or jog
- 4 minutes CH pace/1 minute slow walk or jog
- 2 minutes CH pace/1 minute slow walk or jog
- 1 minute CH pace/1 minute slow walk or jog
- 10 minutes slow walking or running cool-down

THURSDAY

- 4 miles slow, relaxed run or cross training

FRIDAY

- Off or 2 miles slow, relaxed run

SATURDAY

Long Run:

- 9-mile run

SUNDAY

Off

Nutrition Goal

Make sure at least half of your grains this week are whole grains. Whole grains are rich in nutrients and fiber. Choose foods that list one of the following whole-grain ingredients first on the label's ingredient list: 100 percent whole wheat, brown rice, bulgur, graham flour, oatmeal, whole-grain corn, whole oats, whole rye, or wild rice.

Foods labeled with the words "multigrain," "stone-ground," "100 percent wheat," "cracked wheat," "seven-grain," or "bran" are usually not whole-grain products.

"Now bid me run and I will strive with things impossible."
—Shakespeare

Finding Your Team

In her retelling of the ugly duckling story, Clarissa Pinkola Estes, author of *Women Who Run with the Wolves*, observes, "[W]hen an individual's particular kind of soulfulness, which is both an instinctual and spiritual identity, is surrounded by psychic acknowledgment and acceptance, that person feels life and power as never before. Ascertaining one's own psychic family brings a person vitality and belongingness." I love this. We need to—we must—experience non-judgmental connections for the sake of our well-being.

Where we misplaced swans find our team of similarly enlightened souls may be different for each of us, but we know that having a sense of belonging and contributing to a vibrant community are strongly associated with greater happiness and longer living. Have you found your "psychic family" yet? Let me tell you how I found one of my communities.

A few years ago, I joined a delightful club called the Marathon Maniacs. The Maniacs are an international group of runners who cheerfully compete with one another for how many 26.2-mile races they can do in any given year or in a lifetime. I wanted to join the club for one simple reason: I'd met some of its members and they were fun. Really fun!

At the starting line of each race I participated in, I saw them clustered together wearing yellow or red jerseys with bold letters proclaiming, "Marathon Maniacs." They high-fived each other and reported how many races they'd competed in, special homage going to those who'd reached milestones like 50 or 100. While I was standing around alone, knowing I might spend the next five hours running in solitude, the Maniacs had found their peeps. I wanted to be a part of a supportive group like that.

Fortunately, the Maniacs are happy to have new members. Fast or slow, thin or bulky, serious or recreational—all runners are welcome, as long as they love to run and can meet the qualification criteria. The quick way to qualify for this loony club is to run back-to-back marathons (one on Saturday and another on Sunday, for example). I took the slow way: three marathons within ninety days. And they let me join.

In my early days of membership, I was too shy to wear my jersey to races, feeling like I really didn't belong with only a measly sixteen marathons under my belt at that point. Then, last year my I took a driving vacation around the southwest of the U.S. to participate in a marathon in Park City, Utah, one weekend and another one in Santa Rosa, California, the next weekend. I decided to wear my Maniac "uniform" so I could be easily identified by other club members. The experience was extraordinary.

From across the parking lot in Park City, I heard a man's voice, "Hey Ponytail Maniac! Get over here." I didn't realize at first the voice was calling out to *me*, but soon I was enveloped by a small group of runners asking me where I was from and how many States I'd run in and where I was on my marathon count. No one ever asked how fast I was or if I was a serious competitor. They only wanted to celebrate that we were all here to reach a mutual goal to run this race.

During the race itself, as the course weaved its way in and around Park City (which sits at an elevation of over 7,000 feet and was therefore quite difficult for someone like me who lives and trains at sea level), several Maniacs passed me, and without fail, they shouted enthusiastic encouragement. By the end of the race, I knew I'd found a true community. I'd been understood, accepted, and enveloped by others who knew my struggle firsthand because it was their struggle, too.

Who are these people in your life? These are the ones who understand your particular variety of soulfulness and can come alongside you to cheer you on, saying, "Hey, you're one of us. We get you, and we're all in this together."

We all need community. When you've been plugging along in this marathon of life for a while, you get tired. Many days can be hard, exhausting work. You've been laboring your whole life to keep your desired pace. And often, on an extra steep hill, fatigue and self-doubt set in. What you need are people who can surround you with "acknowledgement and acceptance," as Dr. Estes says. You need your like-minded soulmates.

If you're struggling to find community, here are a few suggestions:

1. Follow your interests. Join groups and clubs. Writing groups, book clubs, recreational sports teams, genealogical societies, religious associations, knitting circles, and many other groups have open meetings. Give them a chance, even if you're shy.

2. Ask for what you need. Why not be a little bit vulnerable and let people know you're looking for a place of belonging? What do you have to lose?

3. Be brave and keep trying. Breaking in to new communities isn't easy. You've got to have a certain amount of courage to make meaningful connections. If you give up too early, you may not move through the awkward, early stages of relationship to find real connection.

Whatever it takes, may you find your club, your team, your flock—your refuge. There's nothing like knowing you belong somewhere. Don't stop looking until you find out where that is.

Putting It Into Practice

Intention Word: Accepted

Reflection: Who is in your support community?

Running Mantra: I belong!

Running Focus: During one of your longer runs this week, run with someone who has a slightly faster pace than yours. Push yourself a little to stay with him/her. Just like in life, we sometimes stay at a consistent pace because it is familiar and familiarity is comfortable. Who knows, maybe you'll find your new community and a new pace!

Week 15 Workouts

MONDAY

Speed Workout:

- 10 minutes slow walking or running warm-up
- 1 minute at your current 1-mile pace/1 minute slow
  — Repeat for 25 minutes
- 10 minutes slow walking or running cool-down

TUESDAY

- 4 miles slow, relaxed run

WEDNESDAY

Pacing Workout:

- 10 minutes slow walking or running warm-up
- 10 minutes at your current CH pace/5 minutes slow
  — Repeat 2 times
- 10 minutes slow walking or running cool-down

THURSDAY

- 4 miles slow, relaxed run or cross training

FRIDAY

- Off or 2 miles slow, relaxed run

SATURDAY

Long Run:

- 13-mile run

SUNDAY

Off

Nutrition Goal

This week, ask someone who keeps her body at a healthy weight what and how she eats. Is there someone you admire who always stays at her goal weight in a healthy way? Tell her you admire this about her, and ask if you can interview her and write down what, when, and how she eats. See if you can learn her tricks for staying healthy (not necessarily "thin," just healthy).

Differentiation to the Rescue

You've probably heard the phrase "second wind" so many times in your life that it passes without notice. What does it even mean to catch a second wind? More importantly what does it have to do with you? The second wind is that moment when your energy is renewed. It's the sudden power surge that allows you to keep going even after you've been doing something for so long you've grown weary. And why do you need a second wind? Perhaps you've been running a good race, but you're just plain burned out. Or have you been sick? Maybe you've experienced a catastrophic loss or humiliation and you need to figure out who you are again. A second wind is what happens in that moment when you suddenly find the reserve to plow forward in a way that makes sense and makes you feel alive again.

In a human behavior model known as "Family Systems Theory," the idea of "differentiation" is central. I studied the concept of differentiation in graduate school before I ever started running long distances but running has taught me what the term means on a very experiential level. Let me explain.

Differentiation has to do with how susceptible the "self" is to "group think" or group pressure. The less susceptible to the pressure of others, the higher an individual's differentiation level is. When I first started running races, I felt an expectation to try to keep pace with other runners. Very naturally, there is a culture of competition in most athletic activities;

the point IS to beat other people—or at least beat your own best performance. Running is no different. Race participants are known to keep an eye on and run faster to overtake the ponytail or pair of shoes in front of them.

But for me, competing hard in races doesn't feel healthy. My body just wasn't built for competitive running, and I was (am) totally unable to keep up with most of my runner friends. For me, running has never been about racing and has always been about breathing. Even during an actual event, I want to find an enlightened balance between working my body hard and feeling peaceful. After only my first few races, I realized I wasn't like my competitive pals. In my early days of participating in events, and on the verge of total discouragement, I had to make a choice: Find my own pace and embrace it with pride, or stop running out of shame I couldn't meet a standard that wasn't mine to start with.

I chose to keep running at my own slow, back-of-the-pack pace and to hold my head high even when I was the last to make it to the finish line. I call this kind of differentiation "finding my internal locus of celebration" because sometimes, at the end of a race, no one else is left for me to celebrate my accomplishment with.

Lessons about differentiating ourselves from the pressure to meet others' standards or keep pace with them are important ones because a high level of differentiation means a strong sense of self. After a significant loss or a long, tiring endeavor (like raising and launching children, or recovering from bankruptcy, for example), you'll need a strong sense of self if you're going to be able to catch your second wind and move forward.

Here are some thoughts about increasing your level of differentiation so that you have the reserve to draw up a breath and catch your much-needed second wind:

1.   Cultivate your tolerance for going against the crowd. Not all families encourage differentiation. Especially if you come from a family that valued conforming above independent thinking, you may need to practice staying calm when people aren't happy with you. The

next time you make a choice that presumably disappoints someone in your life, try to self-soothe and re-center yourself.

2.   Think through and articulate what you value. If you're clear about what is important to you, you'll be able to draw on these values when the chips are down. I once met a woman who had lost her entire fortune in an ill-placed investment. Although she was devastated and suffered depression following her financial collapse, she also strongly believed that her most significant personal quality was her creativity. She was able to dig into the reserves of her values and climb out of her emotional hole with a renewed commitment to creatively rebuild her life.

3.   Notice when you feel resentful. Resentment can be a sign that you're ignoring your own values and trying to fit in with someone else's agenda. When you feel resentment, take a moment to evaluate if you're running at "your own pace" or trying to keep up with the pack. Adjust accordingly and you'll find that your much-needed second wind is only a breath away.

4.   Notice what makes you feel alive and refreshed. Sometimes during a marathon, a short walk break can give me just the rest I need to regroup and move on with renewed energy. Whatever brings you joy, provides a rest, or makes you feel safe and happy can give you perspective and the opportunity to get a nice, deep breath so you can move forward again.

Whatever you're facing—whatever brings you to this place in your life where you need to access your reserves and renew your vigor—may you do so with the highest level of differentiation you can . . . And, as I always say, breathe.

"The challenge and the energy running requires may be a selfish one, but it actually motivates me to be stronger in my relationships."
—Joan Benoit Samuelson, 1984 Olympic gold medalist in the first women's Olympic marathon

Putting It Into Practice

Intention Word: Breathe

Reflection: When have you gotten a "second wind?"

Running Mantra: I feel alive and refreshed!

Running Focus: Breathing is a very important part of your workout (and your life!). During runs, many people like to find a breathing pattern to focus on. This week, try different breathing patterns and focus on what feels best during your various workouts. During a tempo/pacing workout, some people like to do a 3:2 ratio of breathing. This means that you breathe in for 3 steps and breathe out for 2. During speed workouts, some people use a 2:2 ratio. Pay attention to your breathing pattern and remember to practice your belly breathing.

Week 16 Workouts

MONDAY

Hill/Strength Workout:

- 10 minutes slow walking or running warm-up
- Find a gradual-to-steep hill to run up
- 2 minutes at your current 1-mile pace uphill/walk downhill
  — Repeat 6 times
- 10 minutes slow walking or running cool-down

TUESDAY

- 4 miles slow, relaxed run

WEDNESDAY

Tempo Workout:

- 10 minutes slow walking or running warm-up
- 22 minutes at your current CH pace
- 10 minutes slow walking or running cool-down

THURSDAY

- 4 miles slow, relaxed run or cross training

FRIDAY
- Off or 2 miles slow, relaxed run

SATURDAY

Long Run:
- 10-mile run

SUNDAY

Off

Nutrition Goal

This week, try a different recipe with unfamiliar ingredients and spices. We tend to eat the same twenty foods year after year. This week, let's spice it up a bit! Research a new recipe or ask a friend to pass along a favorite unique recipe. Buy unfamiliar foods and spices and see what you think. It may take a little more time to shop and prepare, but you are broadening your food repertoire and opening your mind to a new, fun experience.

"I always loved running . . . it was something you could do by yourself, and under your own power. You could go in any direction, fast or slow as you wanted, fighting the wind if you felt like it, seeking out new sights just on the strength of your feet and the courage of your lungs."
—Paula Radcliffe, Olympic runner

Aversions and Strong Dislikes

I've been thinking lately about the term "aversion." Webster says aversion is, "a strong feeling of dislike, opposition, repugnance, or antipathy." The website viewonbuddhism.org defines aversion as, "an exaggerated wanting to be separated from someone or something." You know this feeling, I'm sure. It's more than a feeling; actually, it's an entire body experience in some cases. My friend has an aversion to lima beans and at the mere mention of this legume, he visibly shudders.

When I first started running, I had an aversion to the rain, to hills, to mud, to running alone, to energy gels, to blowing my nose on the side of the trail, and to other runners who said, "Good for you!" when they ran past me. I had so many aversions, in fact, that every run was an act of great planning as I watched the weather reports and searched for flat routes with restrooms along the way so I could find tissue to relieve my stuffy nose.

As time passed and I gradually exposed myself to all of the things I preferred to avoid, my aversions began to loosen. I often forced myself out the door in my rain gear on a wet day just to see if it was really as miserable as I imagined it would be. And do you know what? It was— sometimes! In my misery, I learned to notice my feelings. "Miserable, cold, unhappy," I would say to myself, as I kept moving through chilly, even heavy, rain.

I began to notice that if I named my experience, let it exist without judging it, and kept running anyhow, the feeling eventually dissipated. All on its own. This noticing and naming is called "mindfulness." Mindfulness is the idea that you attend to, with compassion and non-judgmentalism, whatever your experience is in any given moment. You can allow each moment to exist without evaluating it or trying to make it go away. And in so doing, the burden of your aversions (and the energy you spend on trying to prevent experiencing negative things) lifts.

To me, practicing mindfulness is different from just gutting through something hard. I do that too. There are plenty of rainy days when I make it through my runs with the force of sheer willpower and feel cranky and cold the rest of the day. These are the times when I feel unhappy, then feel mad that I feel unhappy, and then feel guilty for being mad at myself for feeling unhappy.

You know what I'm talking about, right? There is a negative spiral that can happen when you judge every feeling you have as being insufficient or unworthy. In the interest of being kinder and more compassionate to yourself, try this:

Suit up for a short run/walk. Step out the door and take a few deep breaths. Notice the air come into and go out of your lungs. As you proceed on your route, pay attention to the thoughts and feelings that come to mind. What does the air feel like as it enters your body? As it leaves it? And, as you proceed, pay attention for your aversions. What do you resist? Dislike? Wish was different? All you have to do is recognize and name your thoughts and feelings—physical or emotional. Cold. Irritated. Tired. Complaining.

While you're at it, notice your thoughts or feelings about "attachments" too. These are the experiences you're drawn to and would like more of. Go ahead and name those: Appreciating the beauty. Enjoying the wind in my hair.

Both aversions and attachments can cause us a great deal of psychic pain because they take so much energy to manage (we push against aversions and cling tightly to attachments), but they're a normal part of the human experience. The more you practice mindfulness, the more you'll live in the moment—where there is nothing to clutch at and nothing to resist.

Give it a shot.

Putting It Into Practice

Intention Word: Feel

Reflection: Take time to really feel your feelings. Name these feelings.

Running Mantra: I have the right to feel my feelings!

Running Focus: Are you experiencing any pain in certain areas of your body when you run? If so, the first thing to do is to visit your physician. With that said, be sure to ice and stretch the area causing you pain. Ideally, you can ice 3 times per day, 10 minutes per time. (A frozen bag of peas is a perfect ice-pack!) While most people are looking for a quick fix or a pill to alleviate pain, consistent icing and stretching can do wonders.

Week 17 Workouts

MONDAY

Speed Workout:

- 10 minutes slow walking or running warm-up
- 2 minutes at your current 1-mile pace/1 minute slow
  — Repeat for 25 minutes
- 10 minutes slow walking or running cool-down

TUESDAY

- 4 miles slow, relaxed run

WEDNESDAY

Goal Race Pace Workout:

- Go to a track or find a flat 1-mile area using your GPS, then do 10 minutes slow walking or running warm-up
- 1 mile at goal race pace/5-minute walk or slow run
  — Repeat 3 times
- 10 minutes slow walking or running cool-down

THURSDAY

- 5 miles slow, relaxed run or cross training

FRIDAY

- Off or 2 miles slow, relaxed run

SATURDAY

Long Run:

- 14-mile run

SUNDAY

Off

Nutrition Goal

This week, name the feeling you are experiencing before, during, and while you eat. When you start looking for food to eat, what are your feelings at that point? Are you starving, sad, excited, just plain hungry? Also, while you are eating, what are your feelings? Are you enjoying, delighted, regretful? When you are finished eating, what do you feel? Are you satisfied, resentful, angry, content, embarrassed? Once we name these feelings, we can learn more about our relationship with food and make healthy changes.

Anything Worth Doing is Worth Doing Badly

"Anything worth doing is worth doing badly."
—G. K. Chesterton

One of my favorite quotes is from G. K. Chesterton, a Christian philosopher who argued that most of what must be done to make the world go 'round is done by the average Joe who does not do it perfectly—or sometimes even well.

For reasons that may be obvious to those who know me, I love this sentiment. Like many of you, I exited my childhood as a perfectionist, afraid of making mistakes and determined to do everything I undertook as flawlessly as I could. I approached college with a soul-killing effort that left me exhausted, albeit graduating with honors. And in my first marriage, I was guided by religious ideas about gender roles that sucked me (and I would guess, my ex-husband) dry after a decade.

It was an unlikely teacher—the marathon—that taught me, once and for all, to dispense with perfectionism. You see, I don't come from a family of athletes. In my family, aunts, uncles, parents, grandparents—all—have eschewed regular exercise. Even in my own generation, there are very few who played soccer or softball. We just aren't an athletic clan. But in my first year at community college, I took a dance aerobics class and learned that I enjoyed moving my body. For years I happily kept up a moderate routine of exercise. And then, in my mid-thirties, someone challenged me to train for a marathon.

I took the challenge and quickly discovered that my body was not built for running. I slogged along on my training runs, barely managing the effort it took to build up my miles. Even now, after more than a decade of marathoning, I'm no faster than I was when I trained for my first 26.2 race. Unlike in my education, pure will and effort have not made me better at running. I do not run because I'm good at it. I run because of what I get out of it. I get exercise, yes, but I also get time to meditate, a way to challenge myself, a clear, deep breath during stressful times, and a regular reminder that perfection is overrated.

In this life, we sometimes do what we do because we do it well. Other times we partake in an activity or engage in a task because it is worth doing. None of us is perfect at marriage, parenting, work, friendship, or any number of other things we value. Some days, if we are honest, we will admit that we aren't even good at whatever we're doing. Does that mean we close up shop and quit?

I daresay most of us live with the paradox of working toward "excellence" while making do with "good enough." Perfectionism, that pesky drive to meet some pinnacle of an outwardly defined ideal, is a mean taskmaster. For those it does not drive into flurries of striving, it often paralyzes.

Think about this: What do you enjoy, but happen to do badly? Whatever it is, I encourage you to do it regularly. Do you love to sing, but can't carry a tune? I recommend a weekly night of karaoke. Do you like to paint but can't even hold a brush steady? Get yourself a canvas and go for it anyway! Do you enjoy cooking but tend to overcook everything? How about Sunday afternoons at your house for burned brunch? Invite people who will love you no matter what you serve them.

Certainly, set goals and strive toward excellence, but to live a life full of joy, you'll need to embrace whatever you enjoy regardless of your skill level. Don't be afraid of failure. If something is worth doing, it's worth doing badly.

Putting It Into Practice

Intention Word: Good Enough

Reflection: What is good enough to you?

Running Mantra: I am proud of me!

Running Focus: As you run this week, pay attention to your hands. Like every part of your body should be during a run, your hands should be relaxed (not clenched). You can keep them slightly cusped, yet relaxed.

Week 18 Workouts

MONDAY

Speed Workout:

- 10 minutes slow walking or running warm-up
- 30 seconds at your current 1-mile pace/1 minute slow
  — Repeat for 25 minutes
- 10 minutes slow walking or running cool-down

TUESDAY

- 5 miles slow, relaxed run

WEDNESDAY

Consistent Speed as Distance Increases Workout:

- 10 minutes slow walking or running warm-up

Ladder:

- 2 minutes CH pace/1 minute slow walk or jog
- 4 minutes CH pace/1 minute slow walk or jog
- 8 minutes CH pace/1 minute slow walk or jog
- 4 minutes CH pace/1 minute slow walk or jog
- 2 minutes CH pace/1 minute slow walk or jog
- 10 minutes slow walking or running cool-down

THURSDAY

- 5 miles slow, relaxed run or cross training

FRIDAY

- Off or 2 miles slow, relaxed run

SATURDAY

Long Run:

- 10-mile run

SUNDAY

Off

Nutrition Goal

This week, add ONE simple lifestyle change to your nutrition. Here are some ideas to help you get started.

1. Eat a healthy breakfast every day. Start your day with a little protein, fiber, and calcium.

2. Serve your meals on a smaller plate. Your eyes will see a plate overflowing with food and your mind will "think" it's getting a lot of food. Try it!

3. When eating, just eat. This means, try not to eat while watching TV, looking at your phone, reading, driving, or working on the computer. Sit down, put your food on a nice plate, and really enjoy the texture, colors, and flavors.

4. Eat at home more often. A problem with dining out too often is that meals are likely to contain more sodium, sugar, and fat than food you prepare at home.

5. Limit your alcohol, soda, and juice consumption. Let's say that you currently drink a five ounce, standard size glass of red wine each evening. If you replace the 125-calorie glass of wine with a zero-calorie glass of water, you would be saving yourself 45,625 extra calories and losing thirteen pounds in one year!

Swallowing Bugs

Have you ever swallowed a bug? If you participate in outside sports of any kind, I'll bet you have. This weekend I was taking a slow, easy run on a gorgeous trail beside the big lake that serves as our watershed, when suddenly a nasty little bug flew right into my mouth and glommed onto the back of my throat. I coughed and sputtered, gagged and hacked, but I could not get her free; she was too far in.

I knew what I had to do, though the thought of it made my eyes water. I had to swallow her. So I gathered up my wits, took a deep breath and swallowed. Then I did it again. And again. It seemed that no matter how many times I did it, she still wouldn't budge. She was as loathe to go down as I was to make it happen.

Other people on the trail passing in the opposite direction glanced at me suspiciously as I alternated between coughing and swearing. Both the idea and the actual experience of swallowing a bug are very disturbing, if you want to know the truth. I felt I needed to get home immediately and gargle with disinfectant.

Unfortunately, I was three miles out on an out-and-back trail and had to go the same distance I'd already traveled to get back to my car. I had no choice but to keep running (albeit now in the direction of an eventual resolution to my problem—the bottle of water in my trunk). As I did so, given as I am to finding metaphors in my running, I started to think about the psychological bugs I'd swallowed recently—in the form of disturbing events that took me by surprise and upset my sense of calm and well-being.

Two things had happened only the week before which choked me up and disturbed me: I'd had a serious conflict with a good friend that temporarily rattled my faith in my own intuition, and then someone very dear to me had a heart attack (minor, but still . . .). Both events were hard to swallow and left me quite distressed.

You've had similar experiences, haven't you? You're going about your business, reaching the goals that the day has laid out for you when, without warning, something devastating stops your breath from flowing easily, and you have to figure out how to carry on before you've even had the chance to process what has happened. It can be a phone call about your lab results or a sudden shooting pain. Maybe it's an email with bad news or someone serving you papers. Whatever it is, it requires you to stop where you are and change directions. You only hope you can get back to safety without further damage being done.

By the time we hit forty, we're no longer under the illusion that life will be without its bugs—big and small. Even so, each time we receive bad news or are surprised by a negative experience, we sputter and choke before coming to terms with the fact that we now have to integrate this new foreign and unwanted disturbance into our understanding of the world.

Since we know it will happen, is there any way to make choking on bugs easier? I don't believe there is, mainly because what makes unexpected negative experiences so shattering is that they happen suddenly—often while we're feeling serene and stable. I do, however, believe we can improve our resilience: our bounce-back-ability. Here's how:

1. Heal old wounds. Carrying the wounds of old trauma around with you every day is like trying to run a marathon with a broken leg. Make the needed time for and commitment to therapy that will allow you to put the past to rest so you can move forward with relative hope and wholeness.

2. Practice a healthy lifestyle. That's right: eat well, get enough sleep, exercise regularly, and minimize the general drama in your life so you have a baseline of well-being to return to when life surprises you with bad news.

3. Surround yourself with a good support system. No one manages the tough times alone, or at least no one should. Make it a priority during the good times to develop relationships that will support you in the hard times.

There's nothing that can take the shock and horror out of troubling events, but the bugs we swallow in life don't have to paralyze us altogether. We must find ways of integrating new and difficult information so that we can keep moving forward. What choice do we have? We may have just as many miles ahead as we've already run.

"To get to the finish line, you'll have to try lots of different paths."
—Amby Burfoot

Putting It Into Practice

Intention Word: Resilience

Reflection: What patterns do you have that help you to be resilient?

Running Mantra: I am strong and powerful!

Running Focus: As we age, we tend to lose some of our strength. Researchers have found that this does not need to be the case. By adding weight-bearing and weight-lifting exercises to our daily routine, we can have strength throughout our lives. Add a quick, 3-minute hand-weight routine to your daily life. Visit mayoclinic.org and search "weightlifting videos."

Week 19 Workouts

MONDAY

Hill/Strength Workout:

- 10 minutes slow walking or running warm-up
- Find a gradual-to-steep hill to run up
- 90 seconds at your current 1-mile pace uphill/walk downhill
  — Repeat 8 times
- 10 minutes slow walking or running cool-down

TUESDAY

- 5 miles slow, relaxed run

WEDNESDAY

Pacing Workout:

- 10-minute slow running warm-up
- 12 minutes at your current CH pace/5 minutes slow
  — Repeat 2 times
- 10 minutes slow walking or running cool-down

THURSDAY

- 5 miles slow, relaxed run or cross training

FRIDAY

- Off or 2 miles slow, relaxed run

SATURDAY

Long Run:

- 16-mile run

SUNDAY

Off

Nutrition Goal

This week, focus on your pre, post, and during run nutrition.

What to eat BEFORE a workout or race:

- Drink water throughout the day.
- Try to eat the same food consistently before each long training run or walk. Eat this food one hour before your long run or walk.
- On race day, eat at the same time before your competition and the same foods that you've consistently been eating before workouts.

A few foods to try: bananas, nuts, oatmeal, baked potatoes, whole-grain bagels, a peanut-butter-and-jelly sandwich.

What to eat and drink DURING a workout or race:

- Find out what brand of electrolyte drink or gel the race will have at the aid stations and train with this brand to make sure it does not cause your stomach any distress.
- When you are running or walking consistently for over an hour, you will need to replenish your water and electrolytes every fifteen minutes or two miles, whichever comes first.
- A few things to try while working out (try them before race day): water, energy gel, and an energy drink.

What to eat and drink AFTER a workout or race:

- Drink water throughout the day.
- Eat something nutritious within one hour after a workout: fruits, vegetables, and sources of protein.
- Try: chocolate milk, eggs, bananas, whole-grain muffins, apple slices dipped in peanut butter, or baby carrots dipped in yogurt.

When is Quitting a Good Option?

Have you ever gotten halfway through something (a book, dinner, a marriage) and realized you didn't have it in you to finish? Here's what happened to me recently:

I signed up for an out-and-back 50K trail run at Baker Lake in Washington State. I'd wanted to do this particular run for years. It's a beautiful trail which meanders around Baker Lake and offers a view of Mount Baker through every opening in the trees.

The morning of the race was unseasonably gorgeous for fall. Dappled morning sunlight fell through the forest canopy. Since I'm quite a slow runner and expected the 31 miles to take me at least 7.5 hours, I took an early start option, beginning my race with a handful of other back-of-the-packers a full hour before the hard-core runners started.

Trail running is different from road running in that you've got to keep your gaze on the ground. Every root, rock, crack, or irregularity is a tumble waiting to happen, so I kept my eyes glued to the single-track trail, even though I was yearning to watch the sun change Mt. Baker's glacier-topped volcanic body from blue to white to yellow. As the hours passed and I slowly made my way to the turnaround point (exactly halfway at 15.5 miles), I reveled in how free my mind was from any kind of worry or rumination. There was only hopping and dodging and plodding forward over hills and through mostly dry streams. (As a side note, if you haven't tried trail running, it's very Zen! You have to keep your mind so focused on your feet that there's no space in your thoughts for daydreaming or fretting over life's troubles.)

For almost twelve miles I languished in the woods feeling about as happy as a gal can feel until the first of the fast fellows, the competitive ultrarunners who had started an hour after me, caught up. Their determination and stamina left me in awe; I even cheered for the first few who passed me. But soon I was stepping out of their way to let them go by, sometimes coming to a full stop because the trail was too narrow to let us both run on it simultaneously. My rhythm and concentration were completely disrupted. For two very long miles—which took me more than a half an hour—I scrambled to avoid runners coming from behind.

Then, at mile fourteen, I looked up from the careful study of my footfall to see a runner coming straight toward me. The fast folks had already reached the halfway point and were turning around now and heading back the other direction. To avoid a head-on collision, I stepped out of the way of the urgent runner coming at me. As I swerved to the right to let him pass, I caught my foot on a root.

Down the hill I toppled, sliding to a stop a few feet beyond the root that had thwarted me. Quickly, I took inventory of my joints and bones. Fortunately, I'd landed on my fleshy parts and was none the worse for the fall.

Still, when I stood up, I knew that the halfway point would be the end of the road for me that day. I'd had a wonderful, peaceful, long, interesting, and fulfilling trail run, but once I brushed myself off and ascertained that nothing was sprained or broken, I realized I'd gotten everything I needed from the experience. I had run the full length of a trail I'd wanted to traverse for a long time; I'd watched the colors of the fall morning illuminate a beautiful natural environment; and, I'd spent nearly four hours in the woods on a clear, crisp day. I was ready to eat my boiled potatoes, stretch my muscles, and thumb a ride back to the start of the race to cheer on the guy who'd knocked me off the trail as he came across the finish line.

In general, I'm a big believer in finishing what I start. I've completed all of my educational degrees, published two books, and conquered over twenty-five marathons and countless other races (including two 50Ks). I've finished reading hundreds of books, cooking thousands of meals, and talking through more "issues" in my relationships than I care to remember. This was my first DNF ("Did Not Finish").

To say that quitting is an option may be unpopular. Finishing what you start is typically considered a mark of good character, but finishing what you start despite there being good reasons for quitting, may indicate compulsivity, a lack of flexibility.

How do you know if quitting is a good option for whatever you're in the middle of? I'll leave the decision to you, but here are a few questions to ask yourself that may help you make the call:

1. Why did you start? What did you hope you would gain?
2. Have you gotten everything you need out of the experience before coming to the end of it?
3. What are the consequences of finishing? What are the consequences of quitting? Is there any danger to either course of action?
4. What is the story you'll tell yourself and others about finishing? What will the story be if you quit?

Think it over. While your mother was right, and completing what you start is an excellent rule of thumb, it's not always the only valid option in every situation. Life is complicated and requires flexibility.

"I run to be focused, strong, healthy, positive and to reach my goals. Running is about putting one foot in front of the other . . . it doesn't matter how fast or slow I go so long as I go . . . It's about believing in myself and others. Running helps me to face the world with a positive attitude and arms wide open to embrace whatever comes my way. It is about keeping the faith and believing in the power of believing."
—Rose Sporty Diva Coates

Putting It Into Practice

Intention Word: Quality

Reflection: What should you finish? What should you let go?

Running Mantra: I am allowed to fail and succeed!

Running Focus: Keeping our knees healthy is very important for an active life. One way to reduce the pounding to your knees during your daily runs is to keep your feet close to the ground and resist the urge to stride out when picking up your pace. Practice keeping your feet close to the ground (like a shuffle) and keeping your legs beneath you.

Week 20 Workouts

MONDAY

Speed Workout:
- 10 minutes slow walking or running warm-up
- 30 seconds at your current 1-mile pace/1 minute slow walk or jog
- 1 minute at your current 1-mile pace/1 minute slow walk or jog
- 90 seconds at your current 1-mile pace/1 minute slow walk or jog
- 2 minutes at your current 1-mile pace/ 1 minute slow walk or jog
    — Repeat this four-step sequence for a total of 25 minutes
- 10 minutes slow walking or running cool-down

TUESDAY
- 5 miles slow, relaxed run

WEDNESDAY

Tempo Workout:
- 10 minutes slow walking or running warm-up
- 24 minutes at your current CH pace
- 10 minutes slow walking or running cool-down

THURSDAY
- 5 miles slow, relaxed run or cross training

FRIDAY
- Off or 2 miles slow, relaxed run

SATURDAY

Long Run:
- 10-mile run

SUNDAY
Off

Nutrition Goal

Add half a cup of cooked beans or lentils to your diet each day. Beans, lentils, and legumes are high in fiber and filled with nutrients. Eating fiber plays an important role in maintaining a healthy weight and having a healthy lifestyle. Studies show that people who eat high-fiber diets weigh less, have lower LDL blood cholesterol ("bad cholesterol"), and have lower blood pressure than individuals who eat lower-fiber diets. High-fiber diets have even been linked to lower rates of certain types of cancer.

"After running a few marathons I can explain to people why I run. It calms me. I can't imagine not having it in my life. It helps me to sort through things. It's like stepping outside myself and getting a better perspective of who I am. Running helps me focus better, helps me take my life in the direction it needs to go. It's not like I concentrate on these topics while I'm in the process of running, but running opens my mind to all kinds of possibilities and perhaps the solution is out there waiting for me to find it. Running takes me to that place."
—Gail Kislevitz, *First Marathons: Personal Encounters with the 26.2-Mile Monster*

The Trilogy of Your Life

I'm always looking for metaphors that might resonate with clients as they seek to catch a second wind in their lives. And while the metaphor of running strikes my fancy, I'm aware it doesn't resonate for everyone.

I was recently talking with a client who shares both my love of running and my passion for reading. We hit on an interesting metaphor that felt powerful to both of us: The Trilogy. Some stories in literature are so complicated and involved that they require more than one literal book. Think of the *Lord of the Rings* trilogy, or the more contemporary *Hunger Games*. In each book of a trilogy, characters are more fully developed, secrets formerly held tight are disclosed, and plot lines unfold more completely.

What if you thought of your life as a box set of stories? What would each book be called? For me, the first book in my trilogy would be called, *The Swimming Pool: In Which She Creates so Many Boundaries to Make Herself Feel Safe that She Ends up Feeling Restricted* (I like long titles). My second book would be called: *Wind Surfing on a Wild River: In Which She Collaborates with the Elements to Get Her to Where She Wants to Go.* And I hope to call the last book in my trilogy *Back Floating in the Ocean: In Which She is Content to Accept Whatever Gifts the Tide Brings Her Way.*

As you might guess, the first book in my life told the story of a difficult struggle I was engaged in to define myself. Many of us come into our early adult years carrying the definitions that others (family, culture, faith, youthful mistakes) have bestowed on us. Both consciously and uncon-sciously, those who influence our self-images as we grow up layer story upon story on us about who we are, what we're allowed to believe or feel. We do the best we can with those stories, not imagining we have control over them.

Then, for many of us, we have a moment (or series of moments—often in midlife) when we realize those old definitions don't/won't work anymore. We long to move outside of the story of life and personhood we've been reading and re-reading over the years, but sometimes we feel stuck. If you were a girl who learned she should be (and tried hard to be) sugar and spice and everything nice, what do you do when you feel your Inner Bitch emerging from behind your sugary smile, ready to give an un-becoming tongue-lashing to someone who has offended you? You either get out the first book in the trilogy and read it with fury, memorizing the lines that help you remain in your "sugar and spice and everything nice" persona, or you consider the possibility that another story-of-your-life might be emerging.

My client and I wondered together what it would be like to close the first book of her life, the one that was holding her growth hostage and shackling her to shame and guilt. What if, we asked ourselves, she could stick that volume on the shelf and really attend to writing/reading the sec-ond book in the series—one in which she could decide how to define herself in a more life-affirming way? What would the chapters on Love, Self-Control, Perfectionism, and Joy contain that might be different from similarly named subject chapters in Book One?

Why not take the time to consciously entitle the books in your trilogy? Consider the questions below. Write down the answers and share them with us if you're willing. We can learn a great deal from one another about the stories we tell ourselves.

- Even if all the years before this very moment were wonderful and brilliant, you're likely ready to turn the page. What do you call the portion of your life already lived? Give it a name as if it represents the first book in your Life Trilogy.

- How about NOW? What would you like this current book to be called? (Book two if you're in the middle of your life. If you are in your golden years, perhaps you'd like to think of book two in retrospect and move on to naming book three.) Name this book something that represents the way of being in the world you'd like to exemplify in the next twenty-to-forty years.

If this metaphor is working for you, feel free to take it a step further and name the chapters in each book. Knowing what to call our experiences can be a powerful catalyst in creating insight regarding the past and discerning wisdom for our future. Give it a try.

Putting It Into Practice

Intention Word: Live

Reflection: What is the name of the story that you are in now?

Running Mantra: I love my life!

Running Focus: Digestive problems sometimes occur during or after a run. First of all, this is normal! Sometimes diarrhea can be caused by dehydration, so be sure to drink water throughout the day and during and after a workout or race. Diarrhea can also be caused by eating a food your body is not used to eating before a run. This is why it is so important to stay consistent with the foods that you eat before and during your long runs and your race.

Week 21 Workouts

MONDAY

Hill/Strength Workout:

- 10 minutes slow walking or running warm-up
- Find a gradual to steep hill to run up
- 2 minutes at your current 1-mile pace uphill/walk downhill
  — Repeat 6 times
- 10 minutes slow walking or running cool-down

TUESDAY

- 5 miles slow, relaxed run

WEDNESDAY

Goal Race Pace Workout:

- Go to a track or find a flat 1-mile area using your GPS
- 10 minutes slow walking or running warm-up
- 1 mile at Goal Race Pace/5 minute walk or slow run
  — Repeat 4 times
- 10 minutes slow walking or running cool-down

THURSDAY

- 6 miles slow, relaxed run or cross training

FRIDAY

- Off or 2 miles slow, relaxed run

SATURDAY

Long Run:

- 18-mile run

SUNDAY

Off

Nutrition Goal

Drink at least eight cups of water each day this week. Our bodies are made up of 60 percent to 75 percent water. Water carries nutrients throughout our bodies, keeps body temperature constant, and helps digestion. You can get the water your body needs from drinking water, milk, fruit or vegetable juice, and by eating water-based soups and juicy fruits. If you cut back on drinking soda, sport drinks, large amounts of fruit juice, and other sugary drinks, you will eliminate many extra calories. Beverages do not make you feel full, so if you drink a lot of calories, you are likely to consume more calories than you would if you drank only water throughout the day.

Sympathy

Today while I was driving home from my office, I watched a family of baby ducklings waddle across a busy road right near where I often run. The poor things barely made it out of my lane and into the next when an SUV came barreling toward them. I honked my horn good and long and the driver put on her brakes just in time for the creatures to look up, befuddled, into the nose of the vehicles. The SUV had stopped in time, thankfully. Before I could think of what should be done to help these little ones safely across the street, two walkers who had watched the near accident unfold rushed into the center of traffic from the sidewalk, waved their arms to stop oncoming cars in the lane next to the SUV, and shooed the babies onto a nearby construction site (and at least temporarily out of harm's way). Tragedy averted!

I must have been feeling tender because I burst into tears. Life is so fragile, I thought. And how wonderful that I live in a world where beings care about one another—care enough to stop traffic and usher ducks across the road.

This was the second time in only a few days that I'd come in contact with the empathetic side of humanity. On the previous Saturday, while in the first couple of miles of the Anacortes Art Dash Half Marathon, I turned to see another runner down on the ground. When I looked more carefully, I could see that he wasn't moving, and he had a goose egg the size of a golf ball on his forehead. Ten racers stopped in their tracks to help him. One woman took his pulse; someone else called 911 to get an aid car; an Anacortes local hailed a passing bicycle officer by name; I held the man's head up and offered him water. In fairly short order, he came to consciousness and told us his name. And then the sirens of the aid car heralded their arrival.

Eventually, I trusted he was in good hands and ran on . . . changed. How horrible to fall so hard during a race, but how wonderful that so many people prioritized sympathy and human kindness in that split second.

There's a lot of bad news in the world on any given day. And because the work I do as a psychotherapist is to hold conversations about people's trauma and pain, it's easy for me to focus on the hurt that just living inflicts on most of us at some point or another. Sometimes you have to pay close attention to notice the gift we can be to one another and to the world, but it's worth looking for. Don't you think?

What moments of sympathy and humanity have you noticed lately?

"What I love about running is you can meditate while running. It's a peaceful place. You pray and think of the children and what you're doing, and you get through it. The time passes clearly. The first mile is the hardest."
—Sister Mary Elizabeth Lloyd

Putting It Into Practice

Intention Word: Compassion
Reflection: When have you felt compassion?
Running Mantra: I am gentle with myself!
Running Focus: Ninety percent of race preparation is mental. You may have thousands of different thoughts and feeling during a race. It is guaranteed that during at least one moment in your race, you will want to give up. This is normal! How are you going to prepare yourself for this point in the race? One way to distract yourself from these limiting thoughts is to practice positive self-talk and mantras. You can also prepare by recording your voice "talking you through" the race. Prepare yourself to stay mentally strong.

Week 22 Workouts

MONDAY

Speed Workout:
- 10 minutes slow walking or running warm-up
- 1 minute at your current 1-mile pace/1 minute slow
  — Repeat for 25 minutes
- 10 minutes slow walking or running cool-down

TUESDAY
- Off or 2 miles slow

WEDNESDAY

Consistent Speed As Distance Increases Workout:
- 10 minutes slow walking or running warm-up

Ladder:
- 1 minute CH pace/1 minute slow walk or jog
- 3 minutes CH pace/1 minute slow walk or jog
- 10 minutes CH pace/1 minute slow walk or jog
- 3 minutes CH pace/1 minute slow walk or jog
- 1 minute CH pace/1 minute slow walk or jog
- 10 minutes slow walking or running cool-down

THURSDAY
- 6 miles slow, relaxed run or cross training

FRIDAY
- Off or 2 miles slow, relaxed run

SATURDAY

Long Run:
- 10-mile run

SUNDAY
Off

Nutrition Goal

This week, truly enjoy your food. We are constantly connected to our outside world. Multitasking is the new normal. In order to slow down, we need to consciously stop, look, listen, and be. Enjoy the texture, the color, the smell, and the taste. Be present when you eat. If you usually eat while doing other things, make a conscious decision to do one thing at a time this week.

Racing the Clock

Did you see the story in the New York Times about Kathy Martin? She's the sixty-year-old runner who broke track records all around the world. She started running later in life and discovered she had a gift. Each race she participates in is a chance to beat the clock, and she does!

What I love about Kathy is that she's grabbed hold of life and squeezed the juice out of it. She says she wants to be "all used up" by the end of her life, and I understand that sentiment. Today I woke up with the same realization I have many mornings: This could be my last day. I'm not trying to be morbid, but we don't have guarantees about how many days we get.

In the town where I live, there was a tragedy on our waterfront this last year. A boathouse on the harbor caught fire and took a number of vessels with it. On one of those boats lived two people I didn't know, but they were friends of friends of mine and their deaths shook me. Along with everyone else in town, I wanted to hear that they hadn't been on board when the fire struck. We hoped the fact that no one had heard from them didn't mean they'd perished. But the news, when it came, wasn't good.

This loss brought back vivid memories of the night my own house burned down when I was eleven. My family was lucky. The smoke woke us up, and although we couldn't reach any of the doors to get out, we all managed to jump from windows (my brother from the second floor) and survived with only a bit of smoke inhalation. But it was close. And I've lived my life since that scary night informed by the fact of death as an imminent eventuality.

When I wake up every morning, I strive for my day to be filled with what makes me feel vibrant and happy. I don't achieve this every day—I'm sort of given to anxiety, blue feelings, and dark thoughts (especially in the winter)—but like Kathy Martin, I'm racing the clock. How much more authentic can I learn to be before my time is up? How much can I learn about joy? How deeply can I connect with those who love me?

What about you? What makes you feel vibrant and happy? Is it a morning run? Holding your dog or cat on your lap? Watching your children sleep? Making cookies with your grandchildren? Is it eating good food? Creating a piece of art? Worshiping silently beside a still lake?

May you race the clock today with your whole heart and squeeze out of life all it has to offer you.

"There is an expression among even the most advanced runners that getting your shoes on is the hardest part of any workout."
—Kathrine Switzer, first registered woman runner in the Boston Marathon

Putting It Into Practice

Intention Word: Accomplishment

Reflection: When do you feel most alive?

Running Mantra: Today is the best day of my life!

Running Focus: This week, spend some time thinking and writing down your running accomplishments and how far you have come with your training. What are some of the physical and mental feats you have achieved over the last year, five years, and ten years? Keep these accomplishments at the front of your mind when you start to feel tired in your workout and race. Well done!

Week 23 Workout

MONDAY

Hill/Strength Workout:

- 10 minutes slow walking or running warm-up
- Find a gradual to steep hill to run up
- 2 minutes at your current 1-mile pace uphill/walk downhill
  — Repeat 6 times
- 10 minutes slow walking or running cool-down

TUESDAY

- 6 miles slow, relaxed run

WEDNESDAY

Pacing Workout:

- 10 minutes slow walking or running warm-up
- 14 minutes at your current CH pace/5 minutes slow
  — Repeat 2 times
- 10 minutes slow walking or running cool-down

THURSDAY

- 6 miles slow, relaxed run or cross training

FRIDAY

- Off or 2 miles slow, relaxed run

SATURDAY

Long Run:

- 20-mile run

SUNDAY

Off

Nutrition Goal

This week, I eat toward my goal weight. My goal weight: _____

How much time do you spend thinking about your weight? What is your goal weight? Sit for a minute and think how you would feel at this weight. How would you look? How would your body move through this world? What would you do that you are not currently doing?

Try acting "as if" you were already at your goal weight. Start being that ideal person without delay. Make the same food and exercise choices as you would if you were your best self.

Audacity

For Christmas last year, I received the gift of a necklace with the word "Audacity" inscribed on it. A perfect gift at the end of what had been a tough year for me in many respects.

Ah, Christmas! I hate to admit, Christmas has never been my favorite time of year. My early memories of Christmas are a mixture of the frantic but joyful opening of gifts and difficult family fights or tragedies (it was at Christmastime that our house burned down). In my twenties, my then-husband and I did our best to create traditions for ourselves, but we were both from divorced families with designs on our time and could never really settle into a routine. More recent years have seen me vacillating between trying to make the holidays happy for those I love and refusing to participate altogether.

I know I'm not the only one whose relationship with Christmas is, shall we say, volatile. I'm a psychotherapist, after all, and my client hours often increase in November and December as people wrestle with faith, family, and expectations. And, I have plenty of friends who negotiate with exes and in-laws and divorced parents for a little space of their own over the holidays.

Last year, a few days before December 25 and before I received my "Audacity" necklace, I took a nine-mile run along one of my favorite routes. I wanted to get some space to feel the complex feelings that come up for me that time of year. As I ran, the trails were damp with dew from the night before, and I passed at least two dozen other walkers and runners doubtless pre-working off the holiday meals they were about to indulge in. When I hit the part of the trail that intersects with a pleasant neighborhood neatly decorated with holiday lights and cheerful blow-up snow-people, I suddenly started to cry—and couldn't stop. I kept up my pace, hoping I wouldn't see anyone I knew and have to stop to say, "Merry Christmas." Memories of difficult holiday experiences came flooding forward; news stories of violence around the world flashed into my consciousness, making me feel helpless; thoughts of estrangements from people I used to know well closed in on me; and the realization that my grandmother, who died last year and would not be present to gather her large, dysfunctional family together for her annual holiday blitz suddenly dawned on me.

I ran a little harder than usual, letting the cold air on my face remind me that I am a part of a larger whole—an imperfect universe made up of people, animals, trees, wind, governments, pollution, and yes, grief. As I neared my turnaround point, the lump in my throat cleared up a bit, running doing its faithful duty to let me feel and move through the worst of it.

On my way back home, I reflected on how the losses of the year had been followed quickly with joy. One of my besties had a baby. Another one reached weight-loss goals that had been beyond her reach in the past. I spent countless hours enjoying love in my life and playing with the four-legged creatures in my house. And, I got a new book contract to co-edit a book on a topic near to my heart.

As I plugged my way back up the last long hill toward home at the end of my run, it occurred to me that a person has to have a lot of audacity to face life day after day. She has to have the nerve to get up in the morning, knowing that the next hours could just as easily hold joy and bring good news as they could usher in devastation and crushing blows. In fact, each day—in this universe that connects us all—holds both happiness and tragedy.

When I reached my front door, I was done with my cry and was glad I'd gone out, although I'd spent at least an hour trying to talk myself into taking the run in the first place. When you feel blue, burdened with memories or grief, I hope you have the nerve to go out and run through it. Each singular breath you take is really the only one that you can count on.

In my opinion, there's no reason to be afraid of hard feelings, as long as we don't become attached to and hold onto them. And I know of no better way to let them run their course than to run.

Here's to the audacity we need to face each new year head on! Cheers.

Putting It Into Practice

Intention Word: Audacity

Reflection: When did you express your audacity?

Running Mantra: I am audacious!

Running Focus: This week, you are starting your taper. During these next few weeks, you are going to be running less. You have done all of the hard work to get you to your race. Now it is time to let your body replenish and refresh so that on race day, you are ready. You need to have faith that you have put in the hard work and that you are ready. Rest up. And trust.

Week 24 Workouts

MONDAY

No Speed Workout:

- Slow 40-minute recovery walk

TUESDAY

- 4 miles slow, relaxed run or walk

WEDNESDAY

Tempo Workout:

- 10 minutes slow walking or running warm-up
- 26 minutes at your current CH pace
- 10 minutes slow walking or running cool-down

THURSDAY

- 4 miles slow, relaxed run or cross training

FRIDAY

- Off or 2 miles slow, relaxed run

SATURDAY

Long Run:

- 10-mile run

SUNDAY

Off

Nutrition Goal

This week, eat nutritious food that you hate. I hate bananas. I hate the smell and texture. But you know what? I eat a banana every day. They make me feel full. They are full of potassium, fiber, healthy carbs, vitamins, and minerals. Does every food you put in your mouth need to be an exciting experience? Can some of what you eat simply be fuel to your body? What are you willing to do with your diet so that you feel healthy, and thus, happy?

Gratitude

If there was one really great thing my parents did for me as a kid, it was to make sure I grew up in a neighborhood. When I was five, we moved into a house on a suburban street with a cul-de-sac, and we stayed there for the rest of my childhood. Some neighbors came and went, but most were life-ers. This gave me a sense of "place" I've never really been able to replicate—until very recently.

In my early adult years, I bounced around from house to house and job to job, trying to figure out where I belonged and what I should be doing with myself. Then, several years later, I moved back up to Bellingham and onto a little street with a cul-de-sac. Some neighbors come and go, but many are long-termers. My running partner, Julie, lives a few doors down, and my next-door neighbors are a pair of fun, smart, beautiful sisters with whom I ran the Tinkerbell Half Marathon some years back.

Not long ago, I went out for a short run with Fuji, my Boston Terrier. From behind me, I heard someone say, "It's Cami." I turned around to see Carol Frazey and Sharon (Carol's running partner). They slowed to my pace and we chatted for a few minutes before they ran on ahead and left me to my own thoughts. And here's what I was thinking: *I'm grateful today for a community of people who know me by name.* It's easy to be anonymous, and sometimes it's even advantageous, but most days, it's nice to live on a little street with a cul-de-sac and to run on trails where you might see friends.

Who in your community makes you feel known and valued? Why not take a moment to express your appreciation for their investment in your life?

Putting It Into Practice

Intention Word: Grateful

Reflection: What are you grateful for?

Running Mantra: Thank you!

Running Focus: This week, focus on your iron intake. Iron is a trace mineral that helps to carry oxygen in the blood to all parts of your body. This is a very important mineral if you are running! If you are still in your "menstruating years," you need 18 milligrams of iron each day (8 mg if you are post-menopausal, 27 mg if you are pregnant, and 9 mg if you are a nursing mother).

Good iron sources include soybeans, beef, white beans, lentils, spinach, pumpkin seeds, and kidney, lima, and navy beans.

Week 25 Workout

MONDAY

Speed Workout:
- 10 minutes slow walking or running warm-up
- 1 minute at your current 1-mile pace/1 minute slow
  — Repeat for 20 minutes
- 10 minutes slow walking or running cool-down

TUESDAY

- 3 miles slow, relaxed run

WEDNESDAY

Race Goal Pace Workout:
- Go to a track or find a flat 1-mile area using your GPS
- 10 minutes slow walking or running warm-up
- 2 miles at Goal Race Pace/5 minute walk or slow run
  — Repeat 2 times
- 10 minutes slow walking or running cool-down

THURSDAY

- 3 miles slow, relaxed run or cross training

FRIDAY

- Off or 2 miles slow, relaxed run

SATURDAY

Long Run:

- 6-mile run

SUNDAY

Off

"No longer do I run from my demons, but run with them. We pace each other, the past and me. And some days, I go faster."
—Caleb Daniloff in *Running Ransom Road*

Nutrition Goal

This week, invite a friend or group of friends to eat healthier. Studies show that you are as healthy as the average of your five closest friends. Take an inventory and see if this is true. Even if your friends are very healthy, there is always room for improvement. Ask a friend or group of friends to start eating healthier together. Decide how you will keep one another accountable.

"Running has made being depressed impossible. If I'm going through something emotional and just go outside for a run, you can rest assured I'll come back with clarity."
—Alanis Morissette, excerpted from *1,001 Pearls of Runners Wisdom*

Remembering Grandma

I lost one of my grandmothers in 2011, and it hit me pretty hard. Because my parents were so young when I was born, I was raised by a trinity of households: my parents' and those of my two sets of grandparents, who lived nearby. I've always thought of my Grands as more than relatives—they were GRAND parents—parents, only grander. My grandmother, Charlotte, was super grand. She was four feet and eleven inches tall, but she lived a big life—full of vim and vinegar—a spitfire. You didn't cross her without being ready for a fight, but if you were part of her brood, you had a loyal advocate, even when you were in trouble.

Charlotte was seventy-nine years old when she died, but she'd been near death many times in her life. She struggled with gross obesity and ultimately managed it with surgery (one of the first intestinal bypasses ever done), though she was heavy until the end. She'd been in the hospital several times in the decade before she died, diagnosed with congestive heart failure and internal bleeding. I'd said my final goodbyes to her at least twice before. And then she bounced back. She was stubborn.

But on Saturday, June 4, 2011, she was taken to the hospital because of a bout of pneumonia. When my aunt told me the doctors said it was serious, I didn't really believe it. Charlotte had beaten back death so many times that I assumed she'd do it again. I planned to go visit her in the hospital (a two-hour drive), but I didn't feel hurried. I even got up on Sunday and ran a half-marathon on San Juan Island.

The morning of the race was beautiful. As I took the ferry over to the island to pick up my race packet, I felt peaceful, enjoying the sunshine on my bare arms and the promise of summer coming at long last. As I stood at the starting line and even through the first several miles of the (very hilly) scenic course, I thought several times about my Gram, but I wasn't troubled. I focused on my breath and counting my steps up the long, winding inclines of the route. Then, at about mile ten, a thought hit me: "This is it. She won't make it through this one."

She'd grown frail in recent months. She wasn't likely to live through pneumonia. I was in denial to think she would. As I walked through the final aid station on the racecourse, I developed a sense of urgency. I took my water from the volunteer, guzzled it, and picked up my pace—with a purpose. I had to get to her and say goodbye. I'd seen her just a few days earlier on her birthday, but I wanted her to have the peace of mind that she'd said goodbye to as many of her loved ones as could make it to her bedside.

I finished the race and quickly checked my phone messages. My father had called to say that the doctors were removing her oxygen. When I called him back, he held the phone up to her ear so I could talk to her. They didn't think she'd wait for me to catch a ferry and drive the distance to the hospital.

But she did wait. I arrived at about 5:30 p.m., and at 7:23, she took her final breath. Sitting next to my Gram as she passed from this life, I felt a flood of emotions: grief, of course, and emptiness, curiosity about the next life, and worry about how the family would reorganize itself without her. I also felt determination to embrace my own life.

I suppose many of us structure our lives informed by those who come before us. We notice what our parents or grandparents did that we admire, appreciate, or disapprove of, and we act or react accordingly, imitating or adjusting. I don't know about you, but there are dozens of things I'm afraid of; there are tasks I face that I feel inadequate for and goals I have that I can't imagine how I'll reach. But in the presence of death, I remembered that I want to live with audacity and determination, to be true to myself and my values.

It took me a few days after my Gram passed to get out for another run, not because I was sore from the San Juan Island race, but because I'd watched her take her last breath, and every time I breathed deeply I cried. Then, on Thursday of that week, I headed for the trails, meaning to run five miles. After a mile-and-a-half, the grief was there. I turned around and ran home to attend to it. Each day, I pushed a little farther until I could run again without the heaviness. I missed her, but I knew she was ready to go; she'd told me that several times in the past couple of years. And I have her verve for life in my DNA.

What family patterns have you eschewed and rejected only to discover that some of what your predecessors gave you is exactly what you need to carry on?

Putting It Into Practice

Intention Word: Wholehearted
Reflection: How do you live life wholeheartedly?
Running Mantra: I am ready!
Running Focus: You are now ready for your race! Here is a pre-race check-sheet to make sure that you have the essentials.

Pre-Race Preparation

1. Set out clothes for your race the evening before.
2. Pack a bag with an extra set of clothes for after the race (set this next to the door).
3. Put any pre-race and post-race food you will need in a bag (set this next to the door).
4. Make sure that you have pre-race foods available and ready to assemble.
5. Check the directions to the race and the starting time.
6. Relax and put your feet up.

Week 26 Workouts

MONDAY

Speed Workout:

- 10 minutes slow walking or running warm-up
- 30 seconds at your current 1-mile pace/1 minute slow
  — Repeat for 15 minutes
- 10 minutes slow walking or running cool-down

TUESDAY

- 2 miles slow, relaxed run

WEDNESDAY

Taper Workout:

- 10 minutes slow walking or running warm-up
- 15 minutes at your Goal Race Pace
- 10 minutes slow walking or running cool-down

THURSDAY

- 2 miles slow, relaxed run or cross training

FRIDAY

- Off or 1 mile slow, relaxed run

SATURDAY

- MARATHON!!!

SUNDAY

Off

Nutrition Goal

This week, eat with the intention of giving your body energy. Food is our body's energy. I (Carol) have a friend who thinks of food as energy for the body. She is of normal weight and has been for her whole life. Food is not a means of comfort for her. Food is not something to ridicule herself for eating. Food is just food. She says that food is fuel. What if we shift our thinking to see the foods we eat as the fuel needed to help us walk through our days, digest our food, heat our bodies, do our art, sing our songs, and dance into the night? Wow, that's a whole new perspective!

Out of Eight Billion, You Only Need a Few

Don't you hate that sometimes in this life we encounter people who misunderstand us? Perhaps they are family members, people in our community, friends or critics of various kinds. Since *Second Wind* came out so many years ago, I've had emails from many, many readers. Some tell me about unkindness they've faced in their lives. Some have been judged to be lazy because they were overweight; some have been denigrated in abusive relationships for years before they found a way out; and still others have been through dark and difficult times (like the loss of a loved one) and have had to listen to well-meaning (but misunderstanding) people speak clichés to them, which only increased the pain. These same readers have also shared with me how running (or other forms of strenuous exercise) has provided a way to come face-to-face with the self in a fresh way and heal from the pressure to meet other people's standards.

The thing is, there are voices everywhere telling us who to be—or who not to be. The media are typical culprits, pressuring men and women to behave (i.e., spend money) in a certain way, but there are other voices, too. Every family has expectations of its members, and in some families, if you decide those expectations don't fit for you, there are high prices to pay in the form of judgment and pressure to fall into line. Even groups of friends (or church communities, work staffs, or volunteer groups) have implicit agreements about the roles each member gets to play. When you decide to step outside of the norm, other people get anxious. If you don't know what I'm talking about, you've either never stepped outside of the expectations others have for you or you're the only person on the planet who is surrounded by perfectly understanding people who totally support whatever you do and never fail to understand where you're coming from, and I'm happy for you.

The rest of us live in a world where some people on some days cannot see us, do not want to be curious about who we really are and wish we were more like them. I recently read a review of my book from a reader who hated it. They missed the point altogether and accused me of all kinds of things I don't think are true of how I represented myself in the story. So, like you do sometimes, I had to live with being misunderstood.

And how will I do that? Just as you do. We get some time alone on the trails (or in meditation, yoga, hiking, the quiet of a church sanctuary). We remember the irrefutable fact that around eight billion people live on Earth and some of them simply will not get us, like us, or want to be around us. But out of all those eight billion souls, there are likely to be a handful who think we're cool. We run/walk/dance/ride to where those people live, get cheered up, and then get back to our lives, living as authentically as we know how.

If you have had a negative voice intrude on your energy or trajectory recently, don't let it take the wind from your sail. Take heart. You don't need everyone to love you. You only need a few.

"I would tell anyone who is thinking about a marathon to go for it and not fall into the 'I can't' syndrome. For that matter, I would tell anyone to follow their dream. Life is too short. Every day we should reach out as far we can to bring that dream into focus and grab it for all it's worth. I am a true believer in carpe diem—seize the day, squeeze every ounce out of it."
—Gail Kislevitz, *First Marathons: Personal Encounters with the 26.2 Monster*

Putting It Into Practice

Intention Word: Friend
Reflection: Who loves you best? Are you your own best friend?
Running Mantra: I did it!
Running Focus: A good rule-of-thumb to remember is that it takes about one day of rest for each one mile of running. This doesn't mean that you should sit on your behind for 26.2 days. It means that you should walk and run slowly for a while and not do any speed workouts until your legs feel "normal" again. Even if you are feeling good right after your race, if you jump back into the faster workouts, you are at great risk of injury. Take recovery seriously.

Week 26.2 Workouts

- Put your legs up and REST. You deserve it!
- Take relaxing walks and enjoy the glory.

Nutrition Goal

Make a nutrition plan for your next adventure!

About the Authors

Carol Frazey is the author of *The Fit School Diet Plan: 1 Year to a Nutritionally and Physically Fit Life* e-book. She earned an M.S. in Kinesiology from the University of Colorado while working with athletes who would go on to become Olympians. As an undergraduate at Pennsylvania State University, Carol was a member of both the cross-country and track-and-field teams. Carol is president of Fit School, Inc. (teamfitschool.com) where she provides coaching and presentations on finding one's power and well-being through movement. Also, she is currently an elected council member for Whatcom County. Carol has appeared in *Woman's Day*, *Dr. Oz*, *Real Simple*, and *Better Homes and Gardens* magazines. Her mission is to educate and motivate individuals to make small changes each day to live healthier lives . . . and to have fun while doing it! She can be found hiking and running on the trails in Bellingham, Washington.

Cami Ostman is a writing coach and life coach, author of *Second Wind: One Woman's Midlife Quest to Run Seven Marathons on Seven Continents*, and the co-editor of *Beyond Belief: The Secret Lives of Women in Extreme Religion* (Seal Press). Cami holds a Bachelor of Education in English and Theater from Western Washington University and a Master of Science in Marriage and Family Therapy from Seattle Pacific University. She runs a nine-month program to help writers get their books done called The Narrative Project. She is also a dog lover, a wine connoisseur, a runner, and a blogger. Her blogs can be found at 7marathons7continents.com, and psychologyto-day.com/blog/secondwind. Her professional offerings can be found at thenarrativeproject.net. Cami has been reviewed or featured in *O Magazine*, *Adventures Northwest*, *Fitness Magazine*, and *The Atlantic*. She lives in Seattle, Washington, with her four-legged creatures.

CPSIA information can be obtained
at www.ICGtesting.com
Printed in the USA
BVHW040919070122
625371BV00026B/1332